FROM EMPATHY TO EMOTIONAL MANAGEMENT

DEVELOP THE ART OF COMMUNICATION IN RELATIONSHIPS. IMPROVE SELF CONFIDENCE, EMOTIONAL INTELLIGENCE AND SOCIAL SKILLS. TIPS TO REDUCE STRESS AND RELIEVE ANXIETY

INTRODUCTION

Modern society poses challenges and difficulties for health students that forced them to acquire a solid intellectual and technical training together with a versatile personal profile. This professional profile implies, in addition to knowledge profession technicians, personal and interpersonal skills to lead to perform adequate professional performance and adapted to the current characteristics of the working market. Above all, in a society governed by a liberal economic model, which makes the possibility of employability fall on the individual.

Therefore, the personal skills that are required for the performance Professional are diverse, particularly in the treatment of patients or users.

Specifically, the management and regulation of emotions are one of the aspects that have aroused a growing interest in the last decade; in short, we talked about Emotional Intelligence (IE).

Research on the relationship between the terms "emotion" and "Intelligence" is not new, but since Salovey and Mayer (1990) coined the term, the field of study of EI has generated a progressive development of research. At present, the debate around the different approaches Theorists of the construct, its genuine character concerning other intelligence or its similarity with other classic concepts such as personality, self-esteem or states of Mood is still open and supports much of the criticism of its detractors.

Among the different approaches to EI, the original theory created by John Mayer and Peter Salovey (1990), remains the most defended and empirically endorsed. From this model, EI includes a set of skills related to the emotional processing of information. Inaccurately, the most widespread definition considers EI as the ability to perceive, assimilate, understand and regulate one's own emotions and that of others by promoting emotional and intellectual growth.

An emotionally intelligent person is one who can: understand, accept and express your emotions naturally; empathize with emotions of others, evaluating them, recognizing and understanding them; regulate the own emotions, helping not to lose temperance; and finally, use the emotion as a performance facilitator. Some studies point out the relationship between emotional intelligence and some concrete measure of academic performance in science students of the Health; showing EI as an adequate predictor of academic achievement. In conclusion, it could be said that emotional intelligence is the ability to adapt emotionally to a situation correctly and perform on it.

CHAPTER ONE: What Is Empathy

The empathy is not only a lovely skill of communication, sharing and other contacts could be a deep and attitude that has to do with how I choose to stand, to think, to act and to communicate to exist. A skill that cultivates deep confidence and acceptance within us, which improves the quality of contact with those around us.

1.1 What Does This Concept Really Mean?

The term empathy was first introduced by Carl Roger in 1951 and was applied mainly to the educational and psychotherapeutic framework with very positive effects on enhancing one's ability to self-fulfill and therapeutic change. The question is whether empathy can be applied to everyday life with the same successful results.

The empathy in everyday life translated as the art of being able for a while to let your own world and enters want, needs, and feelings of others, seeing through their eyes. That is, to make a true space for the other to be heard, expressed, and existed in the way he wants and decides.

Empathy is a way of deeply listening, interacting, and interacting with the outside world. It involves the unconditional acceptance of the other's diversity, the uncritical attitude that comes from recognizing the value of the other as a person and his ability to act, think and decide in the way that he wants. It may seem easy, but it is not and is not a test sufficient to convince you that this process often requires a deep confrontation with the self.

What Is Empathy?

Empathy is the intention to understand the feelings and emotions, trying to experience objectively and rationally what another person feels. The word empathy is of Greek origin "empátheia," which means "excited."

Empathy makes people help each other. It is closely related to altruism - love and concern for others - and the ability to help.

When an individual manages to feel the pain or suffering of others by putting himself in his place, he awakens the desire to help and act according to moral principles.

The ability to put oneself in the place of the other, which develops through empathy, helps to understand better the behavior in certain circumstances and the way the other makes the decisions.

The empathetic person is characterized by having affinities and identifying with another person. It knows how to listen to others, understand their problems and emotions. When someone says "there was an immediate empathy between us," it means that there was a great connection, an immediate identification.

Empathy is the opposite of antipathy since contact with the other person generates pleasure, joy, and satisfaction. Empathy is a positive attitude that allows us to establish healthy relationships, generating a better coexistence between individuals.

1.2 Do You Have Empathy?

Think about how often in everyday life, you want to impose your will and to tell others how they should act, think, act, and feel. Sometimes when others are talking it may be that you show up to listen but in reality just think about what you will answer, not by really understanding them and listening to them but by correcting them, controlling them, giving them pointing out that they are doing wrong or fixing the problem for you.

Sometimes it is because of this that you may be violently interrupted because you cannot hear something that is incompatible with you, become critical of them, raise your voice, feel negative emotions that may be worse — their form to end up in extreme emotional events and actions.

If you remember the important relationships in your family life, at school, at work you will find that sometimes it can be difficult to put aside your own position, defend your own opinion, the strong need to listen, the need to direct, to corrections, control, feel that you are superior to others. How often do we truly let the important people of our lives be able to express their feelings, attitudes, and opinions freely without feeling that they are being directed, directed, or controlled? How often have significant others allowed us to do so? How often do we give them and give us the right to decide for ourselves the way we want to live, decide, act, and exist?

1.3 What Prevents Us From Acting With Empathy In Our Relationships?

Often the people we interact with tend to have a lot of contradictions with us in the way they think, feel, behave, as well as the way they perceive and sense their reality. People also often tend to see deficiencies in others and not fully understand or ignore their own.

The deficiencies of others often suppress our own needs for love, acceptance, security, and more. Oppression of our deepest needs, desires, and expectations by others can severely disrupt our relationships with them. This is because suppressing needs often creates in us negative emotions and thoughts that are difficult to manage, and as a result, we often express them in an explosive and ineffective way.

Thus, interaction can sometimes be difficult, and unhealthy conflict and communication often occur. If you look more closely, you will realize that this constant attitude is gradually hampering relationships and genuine human communication and communication, and as a result, it will drive away rather than unite. In such a context, how to fit an emotional attitude into life?

1.4 Empathy Goes Through the Path of Self-Knowledge

True empathy in everyday life is a difficult road, continuous and with ups and downs, a destination rather than a given situation. It is a path that is gradually achieved through constant reflection and understanding of the self. The empathy towards others first stems from the cultivation of the ability to hear, to listen, and to accept in ourselves, not as perfect but as beings with weaknesses and strengths.

Empathy in our daily contacts means not only the ability to listen, but the ability to hear when we need to talk, when to remain silent, and the way we communicate in order to become richer through the diversity of others, to experience the relationship and our contact with others, to learn, not to teach, to open up through communication and not to be locked into our rigid world. Only then can we be better able to accept and empathize with others as a whole in our lives, then only can we let go of the ego in you and make our relationships more meaningful, profound and meaningful.

1.5 The Science behind Empathy

1. The neuronal mirror system

The researchers discovered a special group of brain cells responsible for the feeling of compassion. These cells enable us to reflect emotions, to feel each other's pain, fear, or joy. Because we are considered to have hypersensitive neuronal mirrors, we experience the emotions of those around us very strongly. How does this happen? Neuronal mirrors are triggered by external stimuli. For example, if our partner is hurt, we feel hurt ourselves. Our child is crying; we feel sadness too. Our friend is happy; we are happy too. On the contrary, psychopaths and narcissists are thought to have what science calls a "defective emotion disorder." This means that they lack the ability to feel as well as all other people, a feature that may be due to the neuronal mirror dysfunction. We have to be careful with these people because they are unable to give unconditional love.

2. Electromagnetic fields

The second finding is because both the brain and the heart create electromagnetic fields. According to the HeartMath Institute, these fields convey information about people's feelings and thoughts. We are very sensitive to this information and tend to be overwhelmed by its volume and intensity. We also tend to feel more strongly in our bodies the changes in the electromagnetic field of the earth and the sun. Emotions know well that what happens on earth and in the sun affects our mood and energy.

3. Emotional infection

The third finding that helps us understand emotionally is the phenomenon of emotional contagion. Research has shown that many people grab the feelings of those around them. One baby's crying, for example, can trigger a wave of crying in a hospital ward. 'H A person who expresses high stress in the workplace can also spread it to their colleagues. People easily catch the feeling of others belonging to the same group.

4. Increased sensitivity to dopamine

The fourth finding relates to dopamine, a neurotransmitter that enhances neuronal function and is associated with response to pleasure. Research has shown that inbound sentiments tend to be more susceptible to dopamine than inbound ones. Essentially, they need less dopamine to feel happy. This could explain why they feel more comfortable spending time with themselves, reading and meditating while needing less external stimuli such as partying and other crowded gatherings. On the contrary, extroverts are thirsty for dopamine and therefore excited about events. In fact, it never reaches them.

5. Sensitivity

The fifth finding, which I find particularly fascinating, is an extraordinary condition called "emotional reflection." Sensory is a neurological condition in which two different senses are combined in the brain. For example, you see colors while listening to a song or feeling the taste of words. Famous sentiments include Isaac Newton, Billy Joel, and violinist Itzhak Perlman. However, with emotional reflection, people can feel the feelings and physical sensations of others as if they were their own. This is a wonderful neurological explanation of the experience of an emotional one.

Research says: Empathy is the most valuable human quality. With these dizzying rhythms we live in, it's easy to get exhausted. Even so, empathy is the quality that will help us. It will enable us to respect each other even when we disagree. Empathy does not make us emotionally crippled, nor does it deprive us of our critical ability. Instead, it allows us to keep our hearts open, to show tolerance and understanding. It may not always be effective in interpersonal relationships and bringing peace to the world, but I think it's the best solution we have.

CHAPTER TWO: The Dark Side of Empathy

According to a new study, we need to be careful when trying to understand how people feel and think. It is often said that the key to empathy is to try to get into the other's place. On this basis, once we understand the other person's perspective, we can anticipate his feelings and behavior, thereby reducing the gap between ourselves and the other. This "theory of mind " begins to develop from our childhood and accompanies us throughout our lives, helping us to develop our social relationships.

But sometimes it is ineffective to understand each other, and because people cannot read the minds of others, words help us. Specifically, when we ask what we want and the answers we receive for what we ask.

Psychologists have conducted several studies to check whether getting into someone else's "shoes" makes people more accurate in predicting the feelings and thoughts of others. In the surveys, participants were asked to "guess" how someone felt in their eyes or to find out if their smiles were false or not. Some of the participants were given various instructions on how to do it, to concentrate, to empathize with each other, to imitate his or her facial expression so that they could more easily get into position before making predictions about how he or she felt. Others were not instructed.

In the findings of the investigations, there was no difference in the performance of those who received and did not receive the instructions. On the contrary, sometimes those who accepted the instructions did worse, proving that sometimes seeing one another's perspective does not work the way we think. Many times we judge each other's experience based on our own information and use stereotypes that are not accurate. However, when we go into the process of thinking another perspective helps us to be less self-centered, does not confuse our own emotions with the feelings of others and helps us to question the accuracy of our assumptions about each other.

2.1 What Is The Advantage When Looking At Each Other's Perspective?

In other couples surveys, participants were asked to enter their partner's place and guess their preferences or opinion about movies, art, jokes, videos, social issues, or even dress up. They were also asked to answer how confident they feel about their cases and how well they know the person they are dealing with.

Psychologists wanted to study whether in real life, getting into the position of someone we are close to is more expensive. The results showed that again, participants who received some instructions did not do better than those who did not receive them; on the contrary, they did worse sometimes. The time they knew the other person seemed to have no correlation. Although you would assume that when you know the other and get into the position of the other, such as a friend or partner, it will be more accurate and effective, it seems that acquaintance is not helpful.

Of course, these findings do not mean that it is of no value to try to experience the other person's perspective but that it is not worth the effort we give it. Instead of constantly appreciating each other's experiences, we can come closer to him. The findings also show that adopting the other person's perspective enhances social relationships. But this is not always good.

For example, as the lead researcher points out, seeing the perspective of a serial killer or a member of ISIS can make us feel closer to them, but that is not a positive outcome. He also states that psychologists' researchers often interpret their findings through their own value system, their own political beliefs, and their own ethics.

Want to know how someone feels? Just ask him

If putting ourselves in the other's place does not always work correctly, then what is the element that enhances precision in interpersonal understanding? In a recent experiment, psychologists studied another strategy. Before responding, participants were asked to either imagine how the other would feel or to ask him about films, art, or anything else they were asked to answer. Those who gathered more information guessed more accurately each other's preferences.

However, they were not more confident in their predictions about others, thus showing that people value the importance of being in the other's place and underestimate direct communication. People have misunderstood what the most effective strategies to understand others are. Although trusting one's instincts and intuition matters a lot to people, as lead research psychologist says, it often leads to mistakes in the intentions of others.

He also stresses that humans are the most social kind on the planet. The problem is that we think we understand others better than we actually understand them, so we come to conclusions that are not accurate.

He cites an example in which he tried to console one of his best friends whose father died. Because she had lost her parents years ago, she thought she understood her pain. But when he showed his compassion, he blocked himself. Her father's death was unexpected, and she felt no pain but peace. So instead of making the assumption about how she feels, she could just ask her how she feels.

No matter whether we are talking about our own spouse or a politician, we are more likely to really understand him if we simply ask him to explain his point of view and listen to him.

To become good at interpersonal understanding does not require doing good things but becoming a good "journalist."

To learn, that is, to put people in a position where they will answer questions honestly and openly.

CHAPTER THREE: The Importance of Empathy

Carl Rogers (Carl Rogers), the inventor of the person-centered method, established the term empathy. He defined it as the therapist's ability to hear and feel each other's feelings, to perceive the connections and meanings that exist in each other's words and behavior. Empathy encompasses acceptance of the other, total respect of his experience and personality, without interpretation, criticism, and evaluations. It is the warmth and security that the therapist provides the patient with knowing, expressing, and investigating the voices that are within him. The healer is often reluctant to let go and experience this freedom, many times having never experienced it again. But then, having built a relationship of trust, he begins to try and get tested.

Throughout this process-process, the therapist is next to the patient and accompanies him, showing respect, acceptance, and an attitude of empathy. It is important to say that empathy happens in a climate of non-direction, as the goal is to synchronize the therapist with the patient's experience. It is not intended to guide, plan, or accelerate the process. Not used as a technique, it is an attitude for the therapist to help the therapist feel safe, accepted, and to better clarify their experiences.

With a compassionate attitude, we can better respond to the wishes of the patient, as we can know him/her "close" and "within," so in an indirect way we accompany the patient, and after listening to his / her wishes, we intervene to facilitate him/her. The Michel Lobrot, the founder of Non-invasive directional (NDI), varies with Rogers saying that there is not to intervene.

We have a responsibility to intervene but in the direction of the healer!

So being focused on the other, empathetic and listening to his wishes, we can intervene by supporting the patient wherever he wants to go. Through this process, the healer feels the security and support to develop his potential, to try new ways of living, allowing himself and others greater freedom, acceptance, and love.

3.1 How Important Is Empathy In Relationships?

In social language, empathy means the emotional capacity to feel what someone else would feel if they were in the same situation as their own. The ability to understand feelings and emotions trying to experience what the person with whom I relate feels. It is not enough just to project ourselves into the situation one is living in and understanding their pain or suffering intellectually. This is sympathy. Sympathy is an intellectual behavior and empathy is an emotive fusion behavior. Being a sympathetic person is choosing to be in the presence of others, to be considerate, to please them because we have affinities with the situation they are living with and with themselves.

What is empathy for? How important is empathy in our relationships?

First, it is important to say that we are not born empathic but become empathic people. This means that empathy is not a personal trait but a behavior that can be learned. The behavior to put ourselves in the other's shoes, to identify with another person or their situation, to know how to listen to each other and to strive to understand their problems, their difficulties, their emotions and to be useful to others. Empathy is a social, behavioral skill needed to live a positive, pleasurable, fulfilling, and quality relationship.

That said, we come back to the questions. Our attitudes affect people positively or negatively, and we will be affected by their reactions to the behaviors we emit in relation to them. It is a social context of action and consequence between two people in any kind of relationship (family, friendship, dating, and marriage). So empathy serves to acquire and maintain a quality relationship with someone.

The first importance of empathy in relationships is to form bonds with people. Without the bond, no relationship is built and evolves positively. We have no desire to relate to people who do not act attentive, caring, and welcoming to each other. Therefore, we avoid contact with these people and do not bond with them. The second importance of empathy is that through empathy, we can better understand the behavior of others and how someone else makes decisions. This understanding of the other helps us to know how it works, and it helps us to know how we should relate to this person if we are to have a good relationship with him. What she likes, dislikes, what she tolerates or doesn't tolerate, what irritates her or makes her happy... When we meet the person we relate to, we increase the chance of success in the relationship, of feeling happiness, comfort, and well-being. The third importance of empathy is that we have the emotional capacity to help people according to their moral principles. Empathy sensitizes and motivates people to want to approach and help each other.

To be empathic, we must be able to overcome the barriers of selfishness, prejudice, or fear of what is unknown or different. For one person to be able to act empathetically, one has to take attention away from one's own problems and keep one's focus on the other person. This is a big challenge in affective relationships, especially since we live in a society that teaches and motivates people to think first about themselves and meet their needs over the other, when we should really think about each other first, to make them happy — and feeling good.

When we do this, the consequences of our behavior motivate the other to treat us well, to make us happy, to value us, and to love us. As long as the philosophy of life is thinking of yourself, Relationships will continue to be abused and broken, and people will be unhappy in their relationships. Empathy cannot be exercised with the intention of receiving something from the person I am empathetic. Using empathy as a behavioral strategy to receive attention, affection, and help will only trigger frustration, suffering, and distress in the relationship. Empathy works when it is genuine. No one owes you anything for being empathetic with someone. The consequence of being empathic is that we feel good, happy, and satisfied that we have the ability to be helpful to those who need us. When we have this conduct in relationships, we receive much more from the other than we imagine and in a very natural and spontaneous way. This dynamic strengthens relationships.

Therefore, empathy is an indispensable behavior to improve the quality of communication and relationship between people. We can exercise empathy by training ourselves to have and keep a watchful and affectionate eye on the needs of the people with whom we relate to help them. If we want to feel happy and have a successful relationship, we need to be empathic.

3.2 How Important Is Empathy in the Workplace

Work is a great place for empathy. In private and professional life, a guarantee of positive communication is the expression of emotions and needs and a willingness to understand others. Only then can you establish a real relationship that will bring professional success:

Empathic work

We work because we want to meet our needs. Mainly to earn money and ensure a dignified life. The work also allows you to meet other needs: self-development, self-improvement, acceptance, achievement of professional goals and ambitions, being part of the team, and a person appreciated and noticed. When the performance of duties is a source of satisfaction and fulfillment in life, it is no longer just a job, but the fulfillment of our key needs. This gives us a better feeling of well-being. As a result, we are more responsible, independent, and willing to take challenges.

Awareness of own needs supports the fight against the main enemies of communication: expressing needs with violence. When we learn about our expectations and requirements as well as pros and cons, we accept ourselves more and learn to receive criticism without strong emotions. Criticism often becomes a reason for quarrels and misunderstandings at work. Nobody likes to be criticized, but when we accept the imperfections, we realize that the person who criticizes us is not the enemy. Therefore, empathy, i.e., talking about emotions and needs and their acceptance are necessary skills in the workplace. When we look at the issue from a different perspective, we can discover a phenomenal solution to the problem and show off the idea.

It is also important to take full responsibility for your emotions. Each of them is the result of satisfying or not satisfying one of the needs.

Road to empathy at work

To use empathy in the workplace, you have to: speak without judgment - when you are out of control over your emotions and evaluate what you see and hear, you can have a destructive effect on communication. Describe the situation impersonally without any emotional terms. Also, try to empathize with the other person's situation. Therefore, do not judge quickly and on impulse. Emotions tend to be the worst advisor; talk about your feelings and needs - do not hide how you feel, just say directly how the behavior of the other person directly affects you; talk about what to do to make it better - in work and everyday life you need to look for the best solutions, simplify and improve ideas;listen and hear what others are saying - thanks to this you will receive feedback and understand it. An active listener is a good employee because he strives to understand not only himself but also colleagues.

3.3 Empathy to Overcome Differences

We live according to our own experience of reality, with a unique vision of the world. It seems a truth. However, we have a hard time understanding this basic principle of subjectivity: we see the world through our eyes. Our perception is limited by our senses, history, and belief systems, by our temperament and moods. The reality that we assume objective and unilaterally apprehensive is not only biased but constructed from our identity and circumstances.

Therefore, it is essential for our individual development and as a society that we learn to see the world according to the eyes of others. This is only possible through empathy, understood as the ability to interpret and experience the world from the point of view of the other. Empathy, then, is an intentional and active attempt to try to understand the worldview that the other person has, their emotions, thoughts and, ultimately, their reality. A reality that, like ours, is also biased by its identity and history.

Human beings are primarily sociable and in our language and ability to communicate that essence is manifested. But communicating is not just talking, it also implies the possibility of understanding the emotional states of the other. And communication is vital to maintain healthy relationships. For this, it is crucial to give entity to the perception of the other and understand that their vision of reality is as valid as ours, even if we do not share it.

From the neuro-psycho-biological point of view, our ability to empathize is inherent in brain activity. The area that assists in the process of empathy is the right supramarginal gyrus, designed to help us distinguish our emotional state from others, with a fundamental role in our ability to decipher what the other may be feeling. It seems that there is a neuronal synapse system that acts as a mirror, somehow reproducing the behaviors of others.

This could explain why when someone yawns, we yawn too. But this process becomes even more complex when it has to do with emotions, as long as it seems to produce a kind of mimesis or reflex. If we see someone feeling pain or joy, we project that emotion in ourselves, experiencing, in some way, the same feeling. Emotions are contagious, so it is crucial to know your own and understand others.

Brain reactions are marked by unintentional, unconscious processes. To promote empathy and improve relationships, it is necessary to make them conscious and deliberate. In other words, to be truly empathetic, one must go beyond the neurological reflex and make a conscious effort to think beyond oneself.

Like almost anything else, empathy is a habit that can be perfected through practice. The rules of empathy are quite simple and include, for example, observing others. We tend to spend most of our time worried and busy on our own issues, on the phone or the computer or prisoners of our routine. Taking the time to observe others can be a great challenge, but it is crucial to the development of empathy. Observe, look, discover, decode, and try to understand what the other person thinks and feels. See beyond our noses and try to decipher who that other is, what battles he is fighting, how he is, or what happens to him. Moreover, overcome the challenge and ensure that these answers matter to us, really and genuinely. See and appreciate, instead of prejudging, categorizing or denying. Having a healthy curiosity about the other, to build it, not destroy it, that is empathy.

Another essential step to becoming more empathetic is to listen.

HEAR! Most of the time, you show conversations - especially those high pitches or quarrelsome - tend to be more verbal combat than a genuine exchange of ideas, with the interlocutors formulating answers before letting the other finish speaking. Speaking without listening, speaking to respond or counter-argument is very different than listening with empathy. To truly understand what happens to the other, one must learn to stop, listen and take the time to respond, process what the other says and learn to exchange opinions in a healthy and constructive way. Before trying to impose our point of view, let's ask questions to clarify the perspective of the other, trying to understand what he meant, what his motivations are, what he feels, what he believes, what assumptions he has, what experiences led him to be who he is.

Communicating does not imply agreeing, and it is not necessary to share a point of view to understand and recognize it. When we really listen, we can improve and amplify our own interpretation and complete our biased and partial worldview. The disagreement may be a complement to our perceptual incompleteness. It is said that empathy is to put yourself in each other's shoes and think about what I would do instead. However, it is more accurate to understand that empathy is to understand what makes the other in his place.

Another rule of empathy is to be flexible and set aside rigid beliefs. Accept that the opinions of others are as valid as their own. Learning from the other and recognizing other ways of being, thinking and feeling, enriches, and improves our perspectives. It is also important to open and express our thoughts and emotions. For that, it is essential to know yourself, that old Socratic proverb. It may sound unlikely, but, many times, we don't know what we truly think or feel, let alone we can communicate it.

Empathy implies challenging prejudices and stereotypes, without judging the one who is different as an enemy.

It is essential to get out of the "we versus those who think differently" dynamic. These labels not only prevent us from growing as individuals, but they stagnate us as a society.

Empathy is a reciprocal issue, based on mutual understanding, observing and being seen, paying attention, and being heard. No one owns the truth. No one. Moreover, we build the truth among all, despite the discrepancies. After all, there must be something in common that allows us to overcome differences and be able to enrich ourselves with them.

CHAPTER FOUR: Types of Empathy

People with empathy are rare human beings who give the impression that they carry the weight of this world. Their souls are among us for one simple reason, to strike the perfect balance in this universe.

They are the people who care and listen to us. People whose halo shines bright and attracts everyone else. Those who are well aware of the environment around them and cannot stand the wilderness.

A soul with deep empathy in this world offers many benefits and benefits but can sometimes overwhelm a person and leave him or her empty and disoriented.

That is why it is so important to find a way to define and give a name to what we are experiencing in order to better understand our nature and to recognize those who have the same abilities as us.

4.1 These are the types of empathy that are recognized everywhere around us.

1) The pure perceptual empathy

These kinds of separate souls have the ability to simply know something or find the right answer to a question that usually confuses others.

The "lamps" of their imagination are easily lit with sudden vivid ideas constantly. .... It is the intuitive ability of clear knowledge.

2) Naturally receptive empathy

These individuals are known to be very sensitive and perceive the physical suffering of others. They feel our illness and physical pain. They are easily depleted when they are with sick people. The stress, pain, and feelings of others can affect them and easily manifest in their body.

3) Sensitivity to fauna

Someone in this category is recognized for his ability to understand an animal's mental state and emotions to the extent that it can interact and positively influence its behavior.

These individuals have a distinct connection to the animal world, and because of this, they can receive the energy sent by them. They are known to love animals more than humans and to have a deeper mutual understanding of all kinds of animals.

4) Germanic Empathy

It is also called environmental compassion. It represents a person's ability to feel and be miraculously attracted to certain places. People with Germanic Empathy can feel the sadness or happiness that exists in one place.

They are often drawn to old houses, graves or churches for no reason. They feel the spirit of a particular location and the events that have happened. They are very attached to the natural world and mourn the destruction that others are causing.

5) Spiritual Empathy

People with Spiritual Empathy have established a deep connection with the deceased and the supernatural. They have the ability to feel or hear the thoughts or mental impressions of the spiritual world.

They are known to be hypersensitive to the high-frequency actions that some people have.

6) Predictive Empathy

These people have a strong sense of intuition. They have visions of events that are going to happen. Forecasting is the ability to predict a situation that will happen — the power of being able to see something that is not even there and to anticipate it.

These appearances of the future are most often presented in their dreams. They dream of reality. We can still say that they are the creators of their realities.

Their dreams are of two kinds: those in which they can see exactly what is going to happen and those who have signs of a future event.

7) Telepathic Empathy

These individuals have the power to read and decipher one's expressive thoughts.

8) Psychometric Empathy

This kind of empathy is manifested in a person's ability to receive energy, memories, and important information from natural objects such as jewelry, clothing, and photographs.

Having and taking care of these abilities can make a person feel worn out and exhausted. However, it is very important to recognize that the unusual abilities that these people cultivate make the world thrive.

CHAPTER FIVE: How to Develop Empathy and Improve Social Relations

You never have the patience just to sit and listen." "All you always want to do is try to fix things." "You just don't understand how much it hurt when you said that." "Judgments like these and many others verbalized or thought in the context of interpersonal relationships often point to a popular problem: lack of empathy for the other.

Empathy is a condition of functional interpersonal relationships. In personal contexts, including marriages, relationships, friendships and relationships with parents, as well as in professional contexts such as management, professional client, student-teacher and peer relationships, be empathic with Situations of others can promote trust, leading to open and honest communication, thus facilitating the resolution of interpersonal conflicts and constructive change.

In fact, the recent work on emotional intelligence by Daniel Goleman suggests that emotional intelligence, one's emotional quotient (EQ), which includes empathy as a core component, can sometimes be more important than the intelligence quotient (IQ).

The initial investigation carried out by Carl Rogers on the importance of empathy in building trust in psychological and psychotherapeutic relationships, as well as in creating self-report inventories designed to measure the empathy ratio (EQ).

5.1 The Virtue of Being Empathic

First, it is essential to distinguish between empathy as a mental state and empathy as a trait or disposition of the character. The first relates to the second as those who are empathic as one of their character traits will tend to experience states of empathy in relation to the difficulties of others.

As a mental state, empathy implies resonating with what is happening in the subjective world of another. Let's call the person with whom you identify, the goal of your empathy. Now, when you identify with someone, we not only know what the objective is going through, but you also feel it, although, as Rogers would say, "without losing quality" as if," that is, without losing your objectivity as an observer.

Then, a friend of yours has just lost her mother; and, although you may not have lost a father, you can still empathize; So you can know what it would be like to lose a father, you can imagine the harsh reality of not being able to see, trust or experience the love and support of someone who has played such an important role in your life. So you can imagine what it would be like to lose your own father, even if you've never had the real experience.

This is what it means to "put yourself in the shoes of the other person." And so, doing so can lead you to emotionally appreciate the loss as if it had happened to you, again, without losing this quality "as if." The emotional response here will include the somatic sensations that can normally accompany the loss of a loved one, such as a hollow hole in his stomach, a lump in his throat and watery eyes.

Then you will also have certain behavioral tendencies associated with such sadness.

However, some people do not seem to resonate very well with the experiences of others. While they may understand their circumstances, they may not have the required emotional response. Even other people may lack the understanding of what a person may be going through as well. In fact, it can be said that some of us are more empathetic than others, which

FROM EMPATHY TO EMOTIONAL MANAGEMENT

means that some are likely to empathize more often than others.

Keep in mind that by saying that some people are more empathetic, I don't want to say that some people have higher quality empathy experiences than others. As a personality trait, empathy is more like being pregnant, which is like being overweight.

People are not more or less pregnant. They are pregnant or not. In contrast, people may be more or less overweight. Being empathetic does not admit degrees. Or are you being empathic or not.

To the extent that it lacks any of the cognitive, emotional, or behavioral components necessary for empathy, it lacks empathy. Therefore, the person who feels emotionally disturbed by the bad news of another person does not feel empathy if he or she does not really understand or appreciate what the bad news really is; and, conversely, the person who knows and appreciates what has happened, but simply does not feel it, also lacks empathy.

So the question of how to be more empathetic becomes the question of how to more frequently achieve the cognitive, behavioral, and emotional synergy that is involved in empathy.

Also note that empathy is not simply a list of independent cognitive, behavioral and emotional variables; it is a balance of such factors that one is thinking, feeling and inclining to conduct in ways that support each other.

Therefore, there is an interaction between these factors. Therefore, the thought of your friend in such emotional pain provokes your own painful sensations, and these feelings, in turn, inform and transform your thoughts, particularly your qualification or evaluation of what happened ("How can this be Such a good person should suffer like this!")

In addition, people who can be said to be empathic are people who tend to be empathic. That is, empathizing sometimes does not make someone an empathetic person, but telling the truth sometimes makes someone truthful.

Because, an empathetic person, like the truthful person, has a habit of being empathic. That is, when others are suffering, they tend to experience empathy for their difficulties. This does not mean that empathic people should always feel empathy in such cases, and true people should always tell the truth.

However, when the lack of empathic consideration becomes more the rule than the exception, then it is clear that the person in question is not usually willing to empathize.

In addition, the analogy with being truthful is also revealed in another way. Empathy, like truthfulness, can be properly considered a moral virtue. According to Aristotle, moral virtues involve the balance of cognitive, behavioral, and emotional factors. The morally virtuous person is someone who exerts a rational restriction on the indulgences of appetites and actions.

Similarly, an empathic person applies their knowledge of the difficulties of others to report their emotional responses to these situations and acts in line with those enlightened emotions. For example, knowing how someone became homeless: the loss of a job, being evicted from their apartment as a result of not being able to pay the rent, not having an address that affects their ability to find another job, etc. can inform the sadness that one experiences from the plight of the homeless and can help motivate One to do something about it.

Now, Aristotle maintained that one attains virtue through practice. Thus, people learn to be sincere, brave, and simply telling the truth, doing brave things, and treating others fairly. Similarly, being empathetic requires practice. To become empathetic (that is, cultivate the virtue of empathy), you must work on it by being empathetic.

5.2 How to Be Empathic

1. **Focus your attention on the well-being, interests, and needs of others.**

As stated, there is a cognitive component to empathize with another. That is, there is some knowledge that you must have to empathize with the other person. First, one does not simply sympathize with another person; rather an empathy with another about something.

That which is what empathy is all about can be properly called the subject of empathy. Now, the issue of empathy is always an event or state of affairs that is contrary to the welfare, interests or needs of the objective.

By "welfare" meaning the promotion of happiness (pleasure and absence of pain and suffering). By "interests" I mean desires and goals held seriously, and life plans, and rights. By "needs" I mean things like food, clothing, and shelter. (Non-physical "needs", such as love, intimacy, freedom, autonomy, friendship, and belonging, include them in interests.)

Any event that affects or affects the welfare, interests, and needs of others also counts as relevant knowledge to empathize.

Therefore, if you know that another has lost a loved one, this fact counts as relevant knowledge; but also, if you know that the beloved was killed by a drunk driver, that fact is also relevant. Why? It is because this fact explains the loss.

In fact, the fact that this individual has been hit by such an unexpected, unnecessary and unforeseen act helps clarify how traumatic the event should be for the purpose. Therefore, the subject of empathy always consists of facts (or claims of facts) about any event or state of things adverse to the welfare, interests or needs of the objective, including the facts (or claims of facts) relevant to this adversity.

2. Key in shared human values.

Such an ability to enter the welfare, interests, and needs of others also requires the ability to take the perspective of another person's value. For example, most of us can appreciate the difficulty of losing a dear relative.

But what if the beloved family member is a pet, say a goldfish? Here, even if you don't regret the death of a goldfish yourself, you may still know how it feels to lose someone you love, so your empathy powers can extend to the loss of the target.

In a general sense, the issue of empathy, in this case, is about the loss of a loved one, which is a shared human value. Similarly, one does not need to be gay to empathize with a gay person about their partner's sexual infidelity. Empathy, therefore, implies the ability to enter shared human values in various interpersonal contexts and cultures.

This value dimension of empathy is an integral part of the emotional component of empathy. By simply understanding the facts related to the subject of empathy, one is not involved in the subjective world of the objective. One cannot feel what is happening.

To be empathetic, you must also "feel bad" about the plight of the target. Here they are not simply entertaining facts; you are also rating or evaluating them. You are evaluating the evil of what is happening in the objective: the suffering, the anguish of not being accepted by your partners; the loss of a loved one; the painful understanding that the love of life has been unfaithful; the fear of losing one's livelihood; the frustration of repeatedly having bad luck; and so.

To get to this place, you must identify with misfortune in terms of the shared human values that are at stake. This is where you put yourself in the place of the objective and imagine how you would feel if you were facing an identical situation.

From this phenomenological position, you are not yet the other person, but you are still (psychologically) there, facing the same adversity. From this perspective, you can appreciate what the objective is going through because now you share the misfortune. Their evil is now evident from this shared, interpersonal and phenomenological perspective.

3. Suspend your own judgments and criticisms considered.

The pronouncements and clichés about overcoming it and moving forward will not bring it closer to the subjective world of the objective. You will not feel pain or anguish, Or the tension in your own muscles. To do this, you must do without your own analysis and criticism, and you should not focus on how to fix things.

In this sense, empathy is antipragmatic. If you approach the goal with an eye on fixing what is wrong, then you will not share the experience of what is (or seems to be) wrong. You will miss the opportunity to empathize. Also, people who are suffering may not even want their confidants to help fix anything, at least not yet.

They may simply want someone to know what they are going through. The solution to the problem may arise after empathy has helped establish a good relationship and trust.

This does not mean that you must accept or accept the perspective of the objective or its value assessments; however, in the process of empathy, you must dispense with your own qualifications, analysis, evaluations, and criticisms to obtain subjective access to the subjective world of the objective.

Of course, this can be very difficult if the subjective world of the objective is perverse or bad. This is the reason why most of us lack empathy for child molesters and mass murderers.

4. Connect with the target.

Suspend your own value judgments, while placing yourself in the subjective shoes of the objective, is essential to empathize. This mental approach is what feminist psychologist Blythe Clinche calls "connected knowledge"..

 The heart of connected knowledge is the imaginative attachment: try to get behind the other person's eyes and "look at it from that person's point of view." You must suspend your disbelief, set aside your opinions, try to see the logic in the idea. Ultimately, it is not necessary to agree with it. But while you're entertaining it, you should ... "say yes." You must empathize with her, feel and think with the person who created her.

To obtain such knowledge, therefore, you must ruin yourself to see the truth in what the objective says. "I can see how difficult it has been for you to overcome your ex; how much you still love her I can appreciate how much you want to be together again and how the idea of her being with someone else is so painful. "

Here you are resonating with the target values. These values (unrequited love, jealousy, sadness and lack of power) are shared human values. As such, it can "connect", on a human level, "with the objective of sharing these values.

This contrasts with what Clinche calls "separate knowledge," which approaches the target with doubt and disbelief to deny what it is saying. "I don't see how you can continue to love her after what she has done to you. What he needs now is to get a good lawyer so he doesn't take it to clean. "

By adopting this last approach, you will not feel empathy; you will not enter the subjective world of the objective; instead, you will analyze it, criticize it and analyze it from the outside. It will probably also alienate the other, who, in turn, will not want to reveal private, personal and intimate details of his subjective life.

However, by adopting the previous approach, that of connected knowledge, you will gain access to the subjective world of the objective because you will think and feel as if it were your subjective world. At the end of the day, you may not accept the thought of the objective; however, he will have succeeded in exploring the details of them and, therefore, will have reached a more enlightened perspective from which to analyze, criticize and offer advice or advice.

Let's emphasize that separate and connected knowledge are methodological approaches to knowledge. As such, each one has value in its appropriate contexts. Separate knowledge uses techniques such as the devil's advocate and logical refutation.

5. Use the reflection.

Note that the last questions are open, which means they cannot be answered with a yes or no. Consequently, such questions facilitate dialogue and, therefore, help foster understanding. In addition, a device that can further promote empathic understanding is known as reflection.

First presented by the psychologist Carl Rogers as a way to express empathic understanding in the context of counseling, reflection implies trying to clarify what another person is saying by reflecting (not repeating) what an objective is thinking or feeling.

"It seems that you feel very disappointed that you have not received a raise," "It seems that you are thinking that others are judging you negatively when you are wrong. "These questions not only help facilitate the development of the objective of your narrative but also demonstrate that you are listening to it; They also help to involve one as a partner in the exploration of the subjective life of the objective, thus promoting greater clarity and understanding of the narrative. This can increase the potential to "connect" and "enter" into this subjective world instead of seeing it from an external point of view.

6. Listen to the objective.

The reflection aims to improve the understanding of the objective (as well as the understanding of the person who is reflecting) by introducing deeper meanings and implications embedded in the narrative of the objective. It is good if you do that and poor if you do not add anything to what the objective has already said. So saying, "It seems you don't like your father" to someone who just said, "I hate that son of a bitch!" He brings nothing to the table, either cognitively or emotionally.

At most, it is likely to be received with a "No duh." In contrast, the answer: "It seems that you feel that your father was not there for you when you needed him" could open new avenues to expand the narrative. In fact, even if the reflection is wrong, it could help clarify things. But too many inaccurate reflexes can also destroy the prospects of empathizing with the goal.

Listening carefully to the narrative of the objective is therefore essential to produce useful reflections; because it is only through "active" listening (which includes asking open-ended questions as mentioned) that you are more likely to see within the subjective world to capture deeper meanings and implications of what the objective says.

Therefore, if you are in the habit of speaking or lecturing to others, instead of listening to them, you may not be empathetic, unless you make a concerted effort to overcome this habit because it is only through "active" listening (which includes asking open-ended questions as mentioned) that you are more likely to see within the subjective world to capture deeper meanings and implications of what the objective says.

Therefore, if you are in the habit of speaking or lecturing to others, instead of listening to them, you may not be empathetic, unless you make a concerted effort to overcome this habit because it is only through "active" listening (which includes asking open-ended questions as mentioned) that you are more likely to see within the subjective world to capture deeper meanings and implications of what the objective says.

Therefore, if you are in the habit of speaking or lecturing to others, instead of listening to them, you may not be empathetic, unless you make a concerted effort to overcome this habit.

7. Use self-disclosure as appropriate.

One way to not listen carefully is to spend time talking about yourself. In fact, others may not open up and share their private subjective worlds if they have few opportunities to talk about themselves and think that you are more interested in yourself than in them.

However, self-disclosure can be a useful and powerful way to connect with shared values when it is relevant and not excessive. In fact, the self-revelation that your own subjective world brings in proximity to that of the objective can also adorn and improve empathy.

8. Adequately distance oneself from the subjective world of the objective.

Aristotle warned us to look for "the gold mean" between excess and deficiency in matters related to passions. For example, moral virtues such as courage avoid extremes between cowardice and folly; friendship avoids the extremes of rudeness and flattery; and the temperance of insensitivity and complacency.

Similarly, as a moral virtue, empathy can be seen as an average between two extremes: being too far from the subjective world of the objective and too close to it. In fact, if you are worried about your own personal problems of life, then you are not likely to get close enough to the subjective world of the objective to identify with the objective of your problems.

On the other hand, if you get too personally involved in that subjective world, you will lose the Rogerian "as if," thus avoiding the distinction between you and the other. Therefore, the key to resonating with the subjective world of the objective is to avoid both extremes. Say you have been through a mess and are now listening to a friend who is going through a similar divorce.

If you start to see your friend's narrative as your own and start projecting your own emotions of anguish, then your friend's subjective world becomes yours; You no longer have any ability to constructively relate to your friend's plight because it is yours.

Then you get lost in that world, and you drown ineptly in it along with your friend. On the other hand, if you face the difficult situation of your friend with a cold "get over it" and, consequently, you fail to connect with your friend, you will be too far from your friend's subjective world to be very useful. So what is the right distance and how to get there?

9. Practice it!

Of course, when strong emotions come on, it is not always easy to apply such a filter, but that is precisely why empathy requires practice and perseverance to cultivate the right habit. It is also the reason why empathy is a virtue or excellence of being human.

Therefore, I urge you to practice applying these guidelines when a friend, a family member, a significant other, a

FROM EMPATHY TO EMOTIONAL MANAGEMENT

colleague, a client, or another relationship of yours only wants someone to talk to. Since it is not difficult to find such contexts in the mainstream of life, it is quite easy to find the opportunity to practice empathy.

The practice will not make you perfect because nobody is perfect; but it can, in fact, help make you more empathetic. And that, in turn, can be invaluable in improving the quality of their interpersonal relationships.

CHAPTER SIX: Cultivating Empathy in Children

The way parents manage their emotions and respond to different situations plays a key role in their children's behavior and emotional life. Thus, parents with high emotional intelligence act very well on their children, as each expression of emotion is absorbed and adopted by them.

One very important aspect of emotional intelligence is empathy. Empathy means that one can feel and be sensitive to what another person is feeling, coming into position, and understanding their own perspective.

Although many children develop empathy more naturally than other children, the way their parents educate them plays a major role in her cultivation

6.1 What Are The Characteristics Of Children With Empathy?

Children with developed empathy have better social relationships, and on the one hand, they behave in a way that does not hurt those around them and on the other hand they know how to provide comfort to someone in need. They can also rely on their own strengths and react to negative behaviors they see in their environment, such as bullying and aggression in general. Finally, high empathy is also associated with high academic performance, as children who know how to manage their distress or a possible failure control their impulses, feel responsible for their choices, and generally care about learning.

6.2 Developing Empathy in Children

1. The child's brain is taught empathy by imitation and observation

And it owes its extremely sensitive mirror systems. From an early age, you can see how efficiently children imitate certain movements and behaviors of their parents and guardians. They can also quickly read adult intentions and tune in to them. They sense the parent's emotional states and completely unknowingly adapt to them. When an adult is irritated or stressed, the child quickly senses his mood and begins to resonate with him - he becomes, e.g., similarly impatient or anxious.

Children also imitate the attitudes of parents towards themselves and other people. They learn how to deal with difficult emotions. How to communicate with other people, how to respond to their behavior and feelings.

As German neurobiologist Gerald Huther writes: " Thanks to the mirror images of the behavior of people who act as role models, usually reinforced by appropriate guidelines and guidelines, children learn very quickly and extremely effectively how they should behave to fit into the community in which they grow up. Behaviors learned as a result of reflection and imitation become most apparent when it is possible to observe a child in the presence of a, particularly expressive pattern. Then, especially in young children, one can see how much they try to imitate the attitude, facial expressions, and gestures of the authority they admire.

Therefore, it is worth remembering that the way we treat ourselves and other people around us is perceived by a young person as a natural role model. The child notices how a parent or teacher experiences different feelings, even if they are not spoken: whether he can take care of himself and his needs or whether he can be sensitive and sensitive to the feelings of other people (husband, siblings, other students at school, etc.), and then duplicates similar ways of functioning in his everyday life - his contact with himself and with other people. In his brain, behavior patterns that he learns from his surroundings are quickly established...

2. The child learns empathy through self-awareness

Children are constantly looking in the words, gestures, and behavior of parents and teachers for their mirror image. They are convinced in this way that someone looks after them, notices them, considers them important. They want to find out who they are and how they are evaluated by other people. Therefore, the mirror image in the eyes of a parent or teacher is very important for children and adolescents.

The young man is not sure in which direction his personal development path is going, so he often feels anxiety and looks for his own reflection in the world of adults - information about who he can become, what he is strong in and what potential he has. This search takes place unconsciously, but according to brain researchers, it is one of the most important elements in the process of "education." "By the way, the words and behavior of the young man pass information about you, we build a kind of" corridor "opening his way to the future and having the power to some extent self-fulfilling prophecy" - indicates Joachim Bauer.

That is why it is so important to get rid of all assessments and labeling of young people. It is worth not expressing depressing and critical messages because these - instead of strengthening self-esteem and the ability to look at yourself and others empathically - can cause uncertainty, personality disorder, anxiety and withdrawal from social life. Let's accept and love children as they are, respect their qualities and individual predispositions so that they can get to know and learn themselves, believe in their own strength, possibilities and take care of building lasting relationships with other people.

3. The child learns empathy from attentive adults

If young people can experience full mindfulness, sensitivity to their feelings, and all emotions of relationships with adults on a daily basis, they will most likely naturally show similar abilities now and in their adulthood. However, if the environment in which they live turns out to be completely insensitive to their emotional and psychological development, they may have difficulties in experiencing the simplest challenges of everyday life, in interpersonal relationships, and even health problems.

Numerous studies confirm that in children who in the first years did not have an empathic relationship with their loved ones, the risk of emotional instability will be significantly increased, in those who often or for a long period felt during the first five years abandoned, did not experience a strong bond with loved ones or had to deal with the trauma of separation, a greater tendency to fall into depression.

The reason for the unstable relationship with others lies in the lack of ability to show understanding of signals coming from their body language and incorrectly responding to these signals. Empathy is also attention to the gestures, facial expressions, and movements of other people (talking about their limits, needs, and desires). That is why it is worth taking care of friendly communication with children every day - tenderly responding to their emotional needs, each time bending over their emotions and various experiences, calmly talk about what they think and feel, what it can result from and how it can be done in a similar situation in the future.

4. The child and his brain practice empathy in natural communication situations

Research shows that we have the capacity for empathy and a sharp moral sense from the first months of life. As adults, we can use this fact in everyday practice with the child. We can support the development of social features - first, recognize them, then strengthen them by naming them and being open to their full expression.

Very often it happens that when a small child notices that another child or adult is experiencing something unpleasant (they cut, fall or hit) - he completely performs some action unknowingly, which in his opinion could bring relief to the sufferer. For example, he gives a crying child a toy in his hand or approaches a parent with his cuddly toy.

It is worth realizing that a small child at the beginning of his life does not necessarily take into account someone's needs and preferences, because it is associated with abstract thinking, for which the toddler is not yet ready. However, let us appreciate his efforts, explaining the perspective of the other person and the course of the situation. Let's talk about what happened, show gratitude to the child for his form of help, explain what a suffering person can feel and ask together what would be most helpful in a given situation. Let's practice empathy at every step, in ordinary everyday situations, and the child's brain will save all important data and encode it long-term. Later he will process them properly and in the future use them in more complicated but in essence similar circumstances.

The American educator, psychologist and researcher Alison Gopnik has proved that if we regularly draw the child's attention to the needs and intentions of others, helping him understand them, during a natural situation regularly, the child will gradually learn more complex empathic behaviors and begin to give support in getting it's a more adequate way. Therefore, according to researchers, the most appropriate way to develop children's great abilities of altruism and empathy is to assume that they are predisposed to altruism and to support this important feature by noticing, respecting (regardless of how the child shows it) and mature guidance.

CHAPTER SEVEN: Emotional Intelligence - What Is It And What Does It Give Us?

Emotional intelligence (EQ) is the ability of a person to recognize and name their own and someone else's emotional states. It also includes dealing with one's own and other people's emotions, is a very important and desirable social competence.

Emotional intelligence is part of the intelligence quotient, also known as IQ. It includes three levels. The first of these is the awareness of one's own emotions and the emotions of others. Level two is an important ability to manage emotions, e.g., calming down in a stressful situation. This is a very important and valuable skill, desirable in many situations. The third area of emotional intelligence is the ability to use emotions in problem-solving situations, e.g., using empathy in conflict situations and finding a compromise solution.

A person with a high level of emotional intelligence has the ability to make so-called insight into himself. This means that he can see the relationship between his emotions and his behavior and well-being, e.g., trembling hands in a situation of nervousness.

Emotional intelligence and its models

Emotional intelligence is a very important element of human personality equipment. This ability allows us to work on emotions, which is recognizing them. How would we function without the ability to name what we feel? Interestingly, the lack of feeling emotions is called emotional illiteracy or alexithymia.

We also distinguish three models of emotional intelligence. The first of them assumes that emotional intelligence is the ability to understand one's emotions, thanks to which we can direct and control them and the ability to empathize with others. The author of this concept is the well-known psychologist Daniel Goleman, author of many valuable publications on emotional intelligence. Another model includes a thesis on four areas that make up emotional intelligence. They are: perceiving emotions, understanding them, thinking supported by emotions, and the ability to manage emotions. Another model, in turn, changes these areas and adds another. These are inter- and intrapersonal intelligence, mood, adaptation to a new situation, and the ability to cope with stress.

7.1 Emotional Intelligence and Its Components

Emotional intelligence consists of two basic components. The first is psychological competence, i.e., relationships with oneself. They include self-esteem, self-awareness, and self-control. Self-esteem is nothing more than self-esteem and self-confidence. It is also aware of your limitations and disadvantages. Self-awareness is already about emotions and includes recognizing your own emotional states and knowingly experiencing them. Self-control, in turn, is the ability to control your emotions and the ability to cope with stress.

The second component is social competence, relating to relations with the environment. They include five very important abilities. The first is empathy, the most important in understanding emotional intelligence. It means the ability to empathize with other people's emotional states. Another ingredient is persuasion, i.e., the ability to arouse in other desired emotional states or reactions, used, among others, in advertising. Assertiveness is another ability, i.e., the ability to defend one's own opinion without criticizing the position of others. Ability is cooperation, consisting in establishing contacts, creating relationships with people and cooperating with them in achieving a specific goal. The last ability is leadership, i.e., the ability to lead others and motivate them to act.

Many experts also include skill in acting as emotional intelligence. They include adaptive skills, diligence in action and motivation, i.e., commitment to action.

As you can see, emotional intelligence is a multidimensional construct, which means that it includes many factors or modules, as the above models show us. This also translates into its usability.

What Does Emotional Intelligence Consist Of?

Emotional intelligence consists of three basic competences, i.e. abilities. The first is psychological competence, which is responsible for the relationship of a person with himself.

a) Psychological competences

These abilities include:

Self-esteem, i.e. self-esteem - it includes awareness of your pros and cons, as well as making an objective assessment of your capabilities;

Self-awareness, or emotional awareness - is nothing but the awareness of our own emotional states, i.e. what we feel, e.g. "I am angry, happy, scared";

self-control, i.e. self-regulation - it includes the ability to respond to external stimuli with the help of appropriate emotions, as well as the ability to cope with stress and act in accordance with the values adhered to.

b) Social competence

Emotional intelligence also includes social competences, i.e. how we deal with relationships with other people. In this case, we have five abilities, such as:

Empathy or the ability to empathize with the emotional states of others - is a very important and valuable skill, because it allows us to be sensitive towards others, understand what they feel and why they behave in a specific way;

Cooperation - it is the ability to cooperate with others to achieve a common goal, allows us to work effectively and solve problems;

Leadership - in turn, is the ability to efficiently and effectively lead and manage others: their work, activities but also the ability to build a team, acquire followers of their views;

assertiveness - the ability to express one's own views while respecting the views of others; it is an extremely important skill that allows us to be polite but firmly refuses to let others be unpleasant;

Persuasion - this is an important ability that allows you to influence others, namely exerting influence on them, inclining to certain activities, it is also the ability to alleviate disputes.

c) Action competences

The third group of skills is competence to act, i.e. how we perform the tasks entrusted to us. Here, too, three specific skills are distinguished. These are:

Diligence - it is taking responsibility for what we do, performing duties on time and feeling satisfied with the activities performed;

Motivation - it is our commitment to what we do, mobilizing our forces to act for a specific purpose; also includes initiative and creativity in action;

Adaptability - this is a valuable ability nowadays, including the ability to get used to changes in the environment and to respond positively to these changes: it is treating them as a challenge; it is also the ability to work in stressful conditions.

7.2 Features of People with High Emotional Intelligence

How to recognize people with high emotional intelligence? They have certain character traits and action people that allow us to state that these people have very highly developed emotional competences.

- **They talk a lot about emotions.** People with a high level of intelligence have a so-called rich emotional dictionary. This means that they talk a lot about emotions, use their names, name their emotional states.

- **They are curious about people and the world.** These people show great interest in what is happening around, willingly meet these people, are active, and have a lot of passion.

- **They are born optimists.** A characteristic feature of people with high emotional intelligence is optimism, and it is contagious. These people are joyful, sociable.

- **They are empathic and assertive**. People with high emotional intelligence are lucky owners of two extremely important features. These areas already mentioned - empathy and assertiveness.

- **They work well in a group**. People with a high degree of emotional intelligence like and work well in a group. This is due to well-developed cooperation skills, empathy, and leadership skills, but without a tendency to dominate.

- **They adapt well to changes**. Emotional intelligence makes us like changes, accept them, and treat them as a kind of challenge. If someone likes change and lacks routine badly, they certainly have a high level of emotional intelligence.

- **They are willing to act.** People with high emotional intelligence are action-oriented. They are activists who enthusiastically respond to all opportunities for improvement and doing something interesting.

7.3 Emotional Intelligence in Practice and People

We already know what emotional intelligence is and what are its components, but how does it translate into everyday life? It turns out that this ability is necessary for us in many areas of life and clearly facilitates our daily functioning. People with a high level of emotional intelligence are open, free to contact, assertive, willing to cooperate, tolerant, and polite. They are happy to engage in new activities, adapt easily, are not afraid of risk. They endure failure and criticism well. They have a realistic view of reality, can soberly look at each other, seeing their pros and cons. They cope well with stress, react adequately to the situation, are able to control their emotions. As you can easily guess, The abovementioned skills are desired by employers but also allow us to function satisfactorily in relationships or other relationships. But what if we don't have all of these abilities and would like to work on our emotional intelligence?

The characteristics and essence of emotional intelligence make it a key factor in the success and development of healthy interpersonal relationships. People with high levels of this trait can recognize and control their emotions and reactions so that they do not influence their judgment, have a positive attitude, as well as understand other people's emotional state. They can, therefore, make good decisions, face difficult situations successfully, and survive adverse conditions.

These people also take risks, have patience and perseverance, confidence, confidence in their abilities, and are optimistic. In addition, they have the ability to work effectively within a team, communicate effectively with other people, build long-lasting professional and personal relationships, and are even better suited for positions of power. To a large extent, therefore, a person's future success, both in the professional and personal spheres, as well as his life satisfaction and happiness, lie in the development of his emotional intelligence.

7.4 Can Emotional Intelligence Be Learned?

Fortunately, it turns out that emotional intelligence can be improved throughout life. Professional emotional intelligence courses are the most effective today. We can also work independently at home. Let's find a moment for ourselves and our emotions. At this time, let's wonder what emotions we had experienced lately, when and how strong they were. Let's add to this our reactions: "Yesterday I was angry because I had an argument with my fiance. I screamed, I left the house slamming the door." If we can be aware of what we feel, we will be more aware of our emotional states. Then let's go a step further and think about how the people around us feel: "My fiance was also surely angry when we argued, and when I left the house he could be concerned about what was happening to me", let's also read the newspapers and let's call emotions on people's faces in photos. Later, it's worth creating scenarios of behavior, for example, wondering how we would behave in a given situation. Our own training of emotions will certainly bring specific results if it is conducted regularly.

7.5 How to Measure Emotional Intelligence?

Emotional intelligence is measurable and is measured using a series of standardized psychological tools. The most popular is INTE, i.e., the Emotional Intelligence Questionnaire. These capabilities can also be chopped down with a fairly simple KKS test, i.e., the Social Competence Questionnaire. He examines our behavior in a number of social situations, including close contact with others, a situation that requires assertive behavior, and social exposure, e.g., a public appearance. The tests are used in diagnostics, including in therapeutic work, as well as in broadly understood counseling, e.g., in career counseling.

To sum up: emotional intelligence is needed, it can be measured, it can be learned. It turns out that it is worth it because of people with a high level of emotional intelligence function much better both in private and professional life.

CHAPTER EIGHT: How to Develop Emotional Intelligence

1. Developing Emotional Intelligence: Emotional Self-Awareness

Emotional self-awareness means having the ability to recognize, understand one's emotions and mood. It is an intellectual process, and thanks to it, it is possible to establish a relationship between what you feel, how you express yourself, and how other people receive. You should focus on yourself to understand yourself a little better.

Thanks to emotional self-awareness, you can identify the concrete emotional states experienced throughout the day so that you can analyze the effect it has around you; these emotions also interfere with social relationships.

For example, on a day when you are happy about making the most of the plans you have with your best friends, it is possible that in a moment of annoyance, you may tend to distance yourself and see the negative side of others. Emotions, in a way, change the way you see the world around you.

2. How to develop emotional intelligence: emotional self-regulation

Also known as emotional self-control, it implies the ability to control impulses and emotions assertively and concretely to avoid living on primary instincts. Low emotional self-regulation can lead to many conflicts, arguments, and fights with those around you. Over time, it can produce a very negative personal image and alienate your close friendships and relationships.

Thanks to emotional self-control, you can regulate emotional responses by reacting appropriately to the events you face in life so that you can better adapt to your surroundings.

It's about learning to think things through before you speak, rationalizing your emotions to keep them from unfolding and turning into anxiety, or getting your own resources to learn how to manage your behavior and emotions with yourself.

3. How to develop emotional intelligence: motivation

Motivation is the third component of emotional intelligence. It is a psychological process that comprises the ability to direct emotional states to a particular goal or goal, always with a positive focus and a lot of energy. Thanks to motivation, it is also possible to easily recover from life's setbacks, find solutions more effectively and refocus on goals, becoming more persistent and emphatic.

For example, if your goal is to get a good job, you may not be able to do it at first, but thanks to your motivation you will never forget what your goal is and will keep looking for the best path until you reach that goal.

The lack of motivation can be translated as boredom, tiredness, the routine understood as negative form, sadness, among others. On the other hand, having a reason to fight becomes fuel for a living.

4. How to develop emotional intelligence: empathy

Working with emotional intelligence, the fourth element is empathy. When it comes to empathy, we are talking about the famous ability to put oneself in another's place, to recognize people's emotions and feelings. In more extreme cases, live these emotions.

Thanks to this ability, you are able to understand and internalize the emotions of others from the emotional expression these people show you. Be aware because, with the feelings and emotions of those around you, you can see your surroundings from another perspective. Knowing how another person feels through understanding gestures is a skill that fosters mutual understanding and allows you to have more and better interpersonal relationships.

For example, if someone is crying beside you, you may understand that they are suffering from some kind of pain, whether physical or emotional. But knowing that this happens, you have developed the ability to be empathic can feel this pain as yours.

5. How to develop emotional intelligence: social skills

Finally, working with emotional intelligence has the last point, social skills. Understand social skills as a set of skills that allow you to respond appropriately in different contexts and better relate to the people around you. They are the key to good personal and professional development. Thanks to them, you communicate more assertively, making your needs known so that the people who live with you understand better how you feel.

A good example of social ability is a person who keeps calm and knows how to express opinions and emotions calmly, avoiding conflict. You should not confuse social skills with manipulating people, as in this case there are no lies, blackmail, or psychological abuse.

Working with emotional intelligence

Other factors to keep in mind to work on and strengthen your emotional intelligence are:

Be resilient

Resilience is the ability of human beings to be flexible in the face of difficulties that arise during life. You can build and strengthen your resilience when, for example, at a very complicated time in your life you are able to look ahead and project overcoming into the near future by understanding what steps you should take in different ways. areas of your life to reach overcoming. That is, "get out" of yourself, your emotions and work to achieve overcoming.

Be positive

Dealing with life's adversities positively is one of the most important elements of a fulfilling life, knowing how to look at the strengths and learn from any situation makes you stronger and more prepared. This does not mean that you cannot be sad at any time in your life, but knowing how to look at the problem, understanding your feelings, taking action, and being able to learn from it all is critical to a happy life.

To be outgoing

Being able to express feelings is an easier way to develop relationships with people so that they are able to understand what you feel and what your limits are. To achieve this, you should go out with your friends more, meditate, propose to get out of your comfort zone.

Have self-esteem

Having high self-esteem is a great way for personal development as it enhances mental stability, helps you make tough decisions and prevents numerous anxiety problems. With self-love, you can achieve many of the goals you set yourself throughout life and especially address those situations that are fearful and susceptible to failure. For this reason, it is so important to work on self-esteem.

Have self-confidence

As we mentioned earlier, it is important to have a well-structured life goal and goal and trust it. However, if you do not have self-confidence and self-esteem, your project may fail because you will be the first to give up. Work on your self-confidence, be constant and daily, is a process that requires patience but is extremely beneficial to your quality of life. But do not confuse self-confidence with pride.

Face the pressure

Today's world is extremely fast and competitive, both in the personal environment such as having the perfect Instagram life as well as in the professional environment because of having to reach goals at the end of the month proposed by the company. However, you should be calm and clearly analyze the situations that present themselves to you.

It is very necessary that you organize and divide your time in a balanced way according to your personal needs, so you will not feel overwhelmed and will perform better in all areas of your life.

8.1 Benefits of Emotional Intelligence

Emotional intelligence can be the best predictor of success in life, giving a more accurate definition of being intelligent.

People with above-average emotional quotients (EQs) are generally better able to cope with the demands, pressures, and constraints of everyday life. It gives them a better ability to control their environment by allowing them to:

1. Better adapt, that is to know how to implement all the solutions, physiological and behavioral to be in adequacy with the whole of our environment - the climatic conditions, the society, the flora, the resources. Anything that can promote or endanger our existence.

"The species that survive are not the strongest, nor the smartest species, but the ones that best adapt to change" [Charles Darwin]

2. Manage tensions, habitual contributions to the search for performance, and the obligation of result.

Tensions must never become obstacles to our projects, so it is essential to acquire the tools of emotional regulation.

3. Improve understanding of the emotions and feelings of the people we are dealing with and inducing a better quality of listening. This creates a link that will often ease emerging tensions through more effective communication or facilitate conflict resolution.

4. To collaborate better. The ability to collaborate is an important component of emotional intelligence. Like the others, it can be increased. It is possible to develop communication, minimize ego and affect, increase the sense of belonging, and share a common vision.

5. Increase creativity by bringing together in our conscious work area the elements scattered in remote areas of the brain

and giving them a new form. For this, it is necessary to solicit the memories inscribed in our senses, draw on our internal database rich in billions of information. We must also work to determine the most appropriate configuration for the emergence of original concepts by identifying the most productive context, circumstances, postures, the degree of relaxation, receptivity, and concentration.

6. To increase our charisma. "To impose it so as not to have to impose, that is what the charisma is about.

One of the essential components of charisma is seduction.

It is only charismatic who seduces. Either by its appearance (the sign of a healthy genetic heritage), but this may not be enough, either by its qualities and abilities.

It is essential to have a sense of self-confidence, to know how to communicate and to have at least one key skill (talent, humor, culture, etc.). It is also important to have a high social and to be a catalyst for positive emotions.

It can easily be noted that many of these parameters can be developed.

8.2 Emotional Intelligence at Work: The 5 Benefits!

1. Improve thinking

Do you believe that reason and emotion are opposite dimensions on the same scale and are always competing to take control of your actions?

This idea makes sense, but it is not entirely right.

If you notice fear or euphoria ahead of a challenge, for example, you may wonder why this feeling arises.

Use emotion like a compass or map to get new information that your logic doesn't recognize.

Other benefits of Emotional Intelligence in this regard are increased focus and concentration.

This avoids distraction with people making malicious comments or sharing irrelevant news, for example.

You will find that these comments and information have no effect on your life, other than stimulating certain negative emotions.

These emotions can be controlled through Emotional Intelligence.

It also helps you solve problems at work without taking them personally, getting faster and less conflicting solutions.

2. Recognize and avoid "emotional kidnappings".

You usually have:

- Tantrums?

- Fight with the people you love?

- Leave important work aside while watching dozens of silly videos?

Moments like this are called emotional kidnappings - when an emotion controls your behavior, and you only realize it after a while.

One of the benefits of Emotional Intelligence is to realize these moments early on.

By noticing these kidnappings quickly, we can then act!

Once you notice them, control the situation quickly and avoid negative behavior, even when there is strong emotion encouraging it.

This is what we might call emotional freedom.

3. Make better decisions in the company.

Emotional kidnapping is the pinnacle of emotional control, but it goes far beyond that, happening in subtle ways in everyday life.

- Eat a bakery snack before arriving at the company, or a healthy meal?

- Sleep early, or watch another episode of your favorite series?

- Pay the bills, or buy something you don't need, why did your co-workers buy it too?

All these decisions have an emotional component, even though it is our custom to hide them: desire, curiosity, envy, and so on.

Are you a manager? This further increases the importance of acting intelligently.

Only then can you get the best out of each of your employees!

There is no point in charging a collaborator much when he is much stressed.

In this case, you may want to have a quiet conversation with him, try to motivate him or take time for the employee to rest and empty his head.

Emotional Intelligence will help you make better decisions, that is, decisions that meet your long-term goals, not your immediate interests.

4. Build deeper professional relationships.

Recognizing and "managing" your own emotions is a step toward doing this with others and building deeper relationships.

This will enable you to realize what they are feeling, and to respond accordingly - one of the greatest benefits of Emotional Intelligence.

Let's say you arrive at work and find your department mate angry after a problem at work.

This will not always be clear, but the signs will be evident to someone who uses emotional intelligence at work and is able to understand them.

Realizing this emotion, you can help him/her to reduce anger!

Help your colleague have a nice day, for example, instead of getting into a discussion that will deepen the bad feeling, be it his stress or anxiety.

5. Health Benefits.

Developing Emotional Intelligence at work will bring benefits to your physical and emotional health as well.

This will be because we will reduce stress and anxiety by not going headlong into negative situations.

This is one of the most important factors, as they not only steal your concentration, making you angry, but can lead to heart and bowel problems, physical exhaustion, and so on.

Therefore, if you fail to apply emotional intelligence to your work environment, your health may suffer, and your performance and professional relationships may be adversely affected.

By making better decisions, you will also take care of your diet as you will have quality sleep and exercise constantly.

In addition, you will avoid risky behaviors:

- distance that long-awaited job promotion in your area;
- treat someone badly that can hurt you in the company;
- self-medication;
- Carelessness caused by the stress of work.

This will ensure a longer and healthier life!

8.3 Roles Of Emotional Intelligence And Teamwork

More and more organizations are realizing that hard skills testing and personality assessments are just not cutting it as tools to use in selecting new hires. As companies begin to realize the importance of social skills like the ability to collaborate and work with a team, they are now looking for those "emotional intelligence" qualities not only in new candidates but in existing staff as well. Emotional intelligence in team building is an absolute must to get the most out of any group of people and here are 7 reasons why.

1. Self Awareness

It is exceptionally difficult to understand the emotions and motivations of others if you don't know yourself first. Persons with a high emotional intelligence can quickly identify their emotions which is the first step in being able to control or manage them. Self awareness is the basic building block of emotional intelligence.

2. Self control

Being able to recognize your emotion is one thing but being able to control those emotions, particularly in stressful conditions is quite another, The person with a developed EI understands why they feel like they do which gives them an opportunity to examine the emotion rationally and control it.

3. Innate motivational tendencies

Motivation is a key to team momentum and every member plays a role in providing that motivation. Developed EI manifests itself as positive attitude, persistence and a natural support for others. In short it is infectious and others will follow the lead.

4. Empathy

The person with high emotional intelligence has the ability to understand the emotions in another and empathize with them. They understand people of all walks of life and the impact that different cultures have on decision making processes. Understanding these differences allows the person to accept diversity and not have it serve as a barrier to working together effectively.

5. Highly developed social skills

Essential to team members is a high sense of social skills. Being able to resolve conflicts in a mutually acceptable way is critical to the overall success of the team. Well developed social skills can strongly contribute to collaboration and cooperation which in turn will drive productivity.

6. Social interdependence

When a team is created it will create an environment of social interdependence and that can be a good thing or bad depending on how it is managed. If the team leader explains that the group will focus on team goals and requires the input of all team members to be successful, the result is a greater effort to collaborate. However if the team is set up as competitors ie "the first one to sell 100 widgets gets a big bonus' then you have a team that consists of individuals with individual goals.

7. EI and team work

Positive and effective relationships between team members have been demonstrated to be the superior emotional setting to drive results. Members who share a bond both professionally and personally will work harder to achieve success for those for the group than a team where those relationships have not been developed. Developing emotional intelligence through exercises and training can greatly improve the odds of effective team performance.

CHAPTER NINE: Facial expressions: communication without words

Not only what you say but also what you do not say influences how others perceive you. Communication is largely nonverbal. Even if we are unaware, our body is constantly sending signals to which our counterpart reacts. Here, the face plays a special role, because on the emotions of the facial expressions are transmitted. Often enough, one look is enough to see how a fellow human being feels. Even if we become masters of deception in the course of life and in many situations want to hide our true thoughts and feelings, we succeed only to a certain extent. Because of so-called micro-expressions give a price for a short moment, which is really going through our heads. How you correctly interpret facial expressions in others, use them for yourself, and what you recognize, what your counterpart would like to conceal from you...

A short definition

The term facial expressions include different movements of the facial muscles, the eyes, the mouth, the lips, but also the cheeks and the forehead. The decisive factor in facial expressions is that these movements are not due to a specific function, but serve only to express personal emotion.

In principle, therefore, not just every facial irritation is part of the facial expressions. For example, anyone who is chewing or speaking is also moving many facial muscles but does so for a clear purpose.

Mimicry, on the other hand, serves non-verbal communication and is, therefore, an essential aspect of interpersonal relationships. Many people feel better when they see someone else's face because it is easier to judge and to assess their intentions. On the phone, this is not possible, so you can easily deceive the other party here.

This is more difficult with direct eye contact. Often one betrays oneself by the own facial expression or awakens with the other at least doubt. But the facial expressions - especially the eyes and the mouth - can do much more and cover the entire spectrum of human emotions and are able to reproduce this impressively accurate.

You should also distinguish the gestures, which is also used to express emotions, but primarily by the use of the entire body, preferably the slopes and arms are executed. In addition, the gestures are easier to control and can be used deliberately to emphasize certain points or arguments or to demonstrate their own refusal, such as arms crossed.

How do we learn to interpret facial expressions?

Suggest facial expressions each person is able to interpret the facial expressions of another. But why? Hardly anyone has specifically trained in this direction, and this is widely taught neither in school nor at university (except perhaps in a few degree programs).

Much of the facial expressions you get to know in early childhood. Various facial expressions are copied from the parents and linked to emotions, so it is already very early on, what a face looks like that is happy or just angry.

In addition, we learn to interpret facial expressions through different experiences that we make in the course of life. The brain stores what kind of facial expressions person shows, with whom we have quarreled, who is sad or who have looked surprised.

9.1 The Seven Basic Emotions

Actually, man is an expert when it comes to recognizing emotions. Just try it yourself. For example, observe your colleagues at lunchtime or look people in the face a little more closely during a walk. Even if you have never seen a person before, you get an impression of the other person's emotional state within a very short time.

This ability was vital to us in earlier times. She warned us of dangers and made togetherness possible. Because people have always lived together in groups, we had to develop an excellent sense of the inner state of others to create a peaceful community and avoid conflicts.

The psychologist Paul Ekman discovered in the 1960s that certain emotions are the same all over the world and can be understood by anyone. Ekman studied video footage of indigenous peoples and found that most of his facial expressions are familiar to him and that he can associate them with a specific emotion.

He then traveled to Papua New Guinea to substantiate his assumptions. He lived under the isolated tribe of Fore. Ekman studied their facial expressions and showed them pictures of the facial expressions of people of other origins. The fantastic result: Even the tribe members were able to assign an emotion to the facial expressions, although they had never had anything to do with other people.

This Ekman could prove that there are seven basic emotions expressed by a specific facial expression:

1. Surprise

The surprise is the shortest emotional state. When are we surprised? When something unexpected happens, when the course of events suddenly changes. To feel surprised, we must not have the slightest hint of what is going to happen.

The wonder lasts only a few seconds until we understand what happened, then turns into another emotion, which is the reaction to what surprised us. Then we can also exclaim: "What a nice surprise!" Or "What a nasty surprise!" But the wonder itself has nothing positive or negative.

The joy or sorrow we feel comes only later when we realize what happened, for example, that we received an unexpected visit. Since surprise comes unexpectedly, it is theoretically impossible to hide it.

The surprise is different from when something, for example, a sudden noise, catches us off guard and scares us. In this case, it is a simple physical reflex, which is the exact opposite of surprise. Let us contract our faces and close ourselves to protect ourselves. When we are surprised instead, we open the face as much as possible; three areas of the face are clearly involved.

The wide-open eyes are often associated with raised eyebrows or wide-open mouths, or both, but they can also appear alone. When we are surprised, we are literally speechless. The chin relaxes and lowers, and the mouth opens wide: how much, depends on the intensity of the emotion.

The surprise can have different degrees of intensity, easily deducible from the mouth. Eyes and eyebrows remain more or less the same, but the more the mouth opens, the more the person is surprised. When you only see the gaping mouth, the feeling is that of being speechless. It can be an automatic expression of real emotion or an intentional sign. When we want to hide what we feel, we often pretend to be surprised.

But since it is a very short expression, in reality, it cannot hide much. A fake surprise can be exposed because it lasts too long. The surprise is the shortest emotion, and it lasts just a few seconds before turning into something else.

2. Sadness

Sadness is one of the most enduring emotions. It has more or less intense degrees, up to the pain that one feels for mourning. All emotions have extreme forms (for example, an exaggerated fear is called a phobia). But here we talk about everyday expressions.

Many factors can make us sad; one of the most common is to lose something. It may be a matter of losing your job, losing a friend or partner, mourning, etc. Sadness also has a social function: those who show that they are sad can get help, consolation, and support from others.

For some reason, we all grew up with the idea that we shouldn't show that we are sad; when they experience this emotion; many do everything to conceal it. But it does not mean that they always succeed because as much as we try to repress an emotion, our face betrays us.

In the most extreme forms, the only sign of sadness can be the total absence of muscular tone in the face. But often the eyes and forehead are also involved. The inner corners of the eyebrows approach and lift. It is one of the most complex muscle movements to perform voluntarily.

The movement of the eyebrows causes vertical wrinkles to appear or stand out above the nose; also, the inner corner of the upper eyelids rises and takes a triangular shape.

A sad mouth is often interpreted as an expression of contempt. The corners of the mouth stretch downwards and/or the lower lip protrude into a grimace. When we feel contempt, we raise our upper lip instead; the corner of the mouth point downwards, but the lower lip is not extended.

If someone is pretending to be sad, he will use his mouth and look down. The absence of expressions of sadness in the eyes, in the eyebrows and on the forehead is a great clue to discover the bluff. To be sure that the expression is authentic, one must observe the upper eyelid in a triangle. If someone tries to conceal sadness, he will try hard to control his mouth.

3. Anger

He feels anger when someone or something prevents us from getting what we want by putting sticks in the wheels. And we get even angrier if the obstacle is designed specifically for us. But we can also be frustrated when things do not work as they should, which is another way of being sabotaged. Sometimes we get angry with ourselves too. Another cause may be violence or threat: then we feel anger and fear together. Obviously, we get angry even with those who treat us poorly and betray us.

Pure anger does not last long, often joins other emotions, like fear and contempt. Anger is the most dangerous emotion because it can lead us to wish to harm, physically or psychologically; the person who made us lose our temper. It is an impulse that manifests itself at an early age and that we must learn to dominate over the years.

It is often best to avoid acting when you are angry because the emotion interferes with our perceptions. In reality, in these cases, it is better to remain still, to shut up and do nothing until the emotion begins to fade, and we start to perceive everything in a more detailed way.

If we suffer some threat, anger causes fear, which can paralyze us, to be halted. Anger, on the other hand, leads us to face danger. When we are angry, the eyebrows approach and lower. This movement in itself can mean several things: the person is angry but tries to hide it; she is slightly irritated and is about to get angry; she is serious and is concentrating; is confused.

If someone makes this gesture while we talk to them, without any problem has occurred, it is the sign that we must explain ourselves more clearly. Darwin called it "the muscle of difficulties," which we use when we are confronted with something complex or incomprehensible.

When you are angry your eyelids tend, and your eyes take on a penetrating look. The lower eyelids may be more or less raised depending on the intensity of the emotion. If someone takes this look without other signs, it means that he is controlling his anger, or that he is trying to concentrate.

To be sure that the expression indicates anger, we must also observe the mouth. There are only two types of angry mouths. That closed with tight lips, which is used during physical confrontations and fighting or when one tries to refrain from saying something, and then open one, which appears when one speaks of one's anger (and when one screams).

The tightened mouth is, however, one of the first signs that appear when one begins to feel anger. It is easy to see the tension along the jaw: it often manifests itself even before we realize we are angry. If someone tries to hide his anger, the tension in his eyelids, his gaze, and his eyebrows will betray him.

4. Fear

Fear is caused by a danger that threatens us physically or psychologically. It is unleashed automatically when some object comes to us quickly, or when we lose our balance and risk falling. Many are afraid of snakes and reptiles or going to the dentist. Fear can affect both the physical and psychological levels.

Biologically, fear makes us ready to hide or escape. Blood flows to the main leg muscles, ready to run if necessary. If we don't run we try to hide, behaving exactly like rabbits caught in car headlights: we remain immobile.

This is because predators with weak eyes do not see prey if it does not move, so the rabbit hides when it remains motionless. When we say "being paralyzed by fear" we are actually hiding.

If we do not run away or hide, the fear is likely to turn into anger that drives us to action to face the threatening situation.

When we are afraid, the eyebrows rise but remain horizontal. The eyes are well opened; the upper eyelids are raised while the lower eyelids are contracted. The mouth is open or ajar, and the lips are tense or thin. If someone pretends to be afraid, he will forget to use his eyebrows and forehead, and probably also his eyes and will simply use his mouth.

The only case in which the forehead and eyebrows are not involved in an expression of genuine fear is when it is a paralyzing emotion, as in the case of a shock. Only the eyes and mouth are involved.

5. Disgust

A distancing characterizes disgust. The most common cause of disgust is bodily secretions: excrement, blood, vomit, and other fluids. The reaction occurs only when they are outside the body. You also feel disgusted with certain odors or when we touch something slimy. Some actions are disgusting like animal violence or pedophilia.

Adults think they are disgusted by the behavior of others: immoral people, politicians, tyrants, etc. But what is morally wrong varies from culture to culture.

The disgust is expressed by the curled nose and the raised upper lip. The lower lip can be raised and extended, tightening the mouth, or lowered and extended, opening it. If the disorder is very strong, the eyebrows can be reduced, but they are not very important in this emotion.

Being an obvious expression, it is easy to pretend disgust, and we often do it to accompany a speech. Since the forehead and eyebrows are not significant for this expression, we do not notice their absence in the case of fake emotion. For this reason, it is an emotion that is easy to mask as it mainly uses the lower part of the face. Usually, we don't even bother to hide this emotion.

6. Contempt

Disdain has much in common with disgust, but there are some essential differences. We feel contempt for others and their actions, but not for things.

There is also a sort of socio-cultural contempt from the bottom up, such as what young people feel towards adults or poorly educated towards academics.

Those who are insecure about their position and status often use contempt as a weapon. Many take advantage of their power to show contempt for those who are subordinate to them. It is a very effective method even if then we find ourselves alone at the top hated by all.

Our face expresses contempt by locking and lifting only one corner of the mouth, like a kind of half-smile and or raising only half of the upper lip, like a half expression of disgust.

It can occur discreetly with a slight trembling of the upper lip, or more intensely, by uncovering the teeth. The eye tends to point down; we look down on the person we despise.

If this expression is a natural part of your face, because you were born that way, you will be easily labeled as arrogant and opinionated.

7. Joy

Positive emotions are numerous but currently, we do not have sufficient terms to describe them. For now, we must be content with words like joy or happiness.

An authentic smile involves two essential muscles: the zygomatic major, which raises the corners of the mouth, and the eyes orbicular that relaxes the area around the eyelids. In this way, the eyes are tightened a little, the skin under the lower eyelids is stretched, the eyebrows are lowered, and folds appear on the sides of the eyes.

We can intentionally control the zygomatic major, but this does not apply to the muscles around the eyes. When this muscle is active, we say that someone "smiles with their eyes." The fact that we are unable to control the eyes orbicular makes it easy to recognize a fake smile. In an authentic smile, the eyebrows are slightly lowered, something that nobody can reproduce voluntarily.

If we don't want to be discovered when we pretend to be happy, we have to make the widest possible smile. Then the changes caused by the eye muscles also take place: a wide smile pushes up the cheeks making the skin curl under the eyes; in this way, the eyelids tighten, and wrinkles appear on the sides. It then becomes more challenging to understand whether the smile is sincere or not: the only indication is the eyebrows and the skin below, which is the eye muscles lower a genuine smile.

Ekman developed a system for deciphering and describing facial expressions. It's called the "Facial Action Coding System," FACS for short, and it describes a total of 44 small facial muscle movements. This system helps to detect emotions and makes it possible to interpret facial expressions.

9.2 Micro-Expressions Show the True Feelings

How do Paul Ekman's findings help in everyday life? In the daily routine, we are programmed to hide our feelings. It is smiled although you are not feeling well. It is agreed, although one feels rejection. But the facial muscles are directly linked to the limbic system, the emotional center. Thus, it is not possible to completely hide their feelings.

In a facial expression shorter than the duration of a blink of an eye, feelings flash for a moment. These are the so-called micro-expressions.

They come to light because the limbic system processes information faster than the cerebrum, thereby tearing us away from controlling one's own emotions for a moment. Uncontrollable reflects on the face for a moment the truth that we really feel. Only then can the mask be put on again.

Especially in situations that touch one emotionally, for example, when it comes to a topic that is important to you, micro expression intensifies. A contradiction in what someone says and what someone thinks and feels is only apparent in this brief moment.

9.3 Mimic Point: Error Reading Faces

We should not underestimate how difficult it can be to read a facial expression correctly. A small muscle movement can have different meanings, and the differences are often minimal, increasing the likelihood of a mistake and illustrating how much exercise may be necessary to interpret the facial expressions of others unerringly.

A complete picture is a combination of facial expressions, gestures, and posture. To properly interpret the countenance of the other person, be sure to avoid these mistakes:

1. **Isolation**

You may have heard that it can be a telltale sign of a lie when someone grabs your narrative. But it could just itch on the nose. Meaning: a single gesture reveals nothing. Only when similar signals accumulate in the facial expressions, it becomes a sign.

So consider a single facial expression never isolated. This merely increases the risk of interpreting something into the other person's facial expression, which is not there at all.

2. Context

Do not just try to interpret the nonverbal language, but always see it in a context: What background has your counterpart? Is the person under particular pressure? Do not you like the room? Or what experiences have the person with such situations already collected?

Depending on the context, facial expressions can mean something different and should be judged accordingly differentiated. Here, it helps to know the other person better to assess the differences in the face between normal behavior and the current situation.

3. Blindness

Do you know the halo effect that was discovered in the 19th century by the American behavioral scientist Edward Lee Thorndike? It describes a perceptual error in which individual characteristics of a person are so dominant on us that they produce an over shining overall impression.

For example, students with glasses look smarter on many teachers. And that's exactly the problem: you always interpret facial expressions through your own glasses - and that can be cloudy if your perception plays a trick on you do not notice.

9.4 Facial Expressions: How Do I Know That My Counterpart Is Keeping Something From Me?

Recognizing this contradiction can help one understand one's counterpart. In the job, this ability is a crucial advantage. For example, talking to a customer about a new suggestion will help you find out if you are positive or negative about it.

Certain signals on the face point you in discussions to objections, doubts, or rejection. However, it should be said in advance that the recognition of these signals requires intensive training. You will not immediately recognize them, if only because they only show up in the face of your counterpart for a fraction of a second.

This signals express doubts and objections:

Raise the eyebrows

If the eyebrows of a conversation partner shoot skyward, this unconscious expresses skepticism. It shows that he is not yet convinced of what you say. It can also be a sign of new life. If the eyebrows are raised only slightly, your counterpart will signal interest.

The lips aprons

This may mean that your correspondent thinks about your proposal and weighs it up. But it can also mean that your opponent is considering another proposal.

The eyebrows contract

This signal is an expression that your counterpart is concentrated. However, if I pull the eyelids up, annoyance is signaled.

This signals express rejection:

Pull up the upper lip

An upper lip shows that your opponent assesses the situation differently than you. Being aware of this while suggesting or explaining something may mean that your interviewee disagrees with you.

The nose up

Even those who sniff the nose signals that something does not suit him. This signal can also mean that your counterpart thinks what you propose is difficult to implement.

If you can observe one of these signals with your correspondent, let this observation flow into the conversation. For example, you could say, I see, you still have doubts. They will talk to the interlocutor and have the chance to convince him. In addition, you prove your empathy.

9.5 Facial Expressions: How She Influences Us

As a non-verbal communication, facial expressions have a very direct influence on how other people perceive and judge us. How much this works, everyone can experience for themselves. Imagine, for example, meeting a new colleague or meeting new people at a party, where the rejection is virtually written in the face. With all the effort, it will hardly succeed to perceive them as sympathetic or even make friends.

It is very different when someone is open, friendly, positive, and inviting facial expressions. It makes you feel welcome, builds a good rapport, and keeps talking. Even a smile and eye contact can be enough to attract fellow human beings and break the ice.

But facial expressions influence not only the behavior and emotions of other people. You can also use your facial expressions in a targeted manner to improve your own mood or even become more self-confident. How does it work? Simple: smile - even if you have no reason to.

Whether you feel like a smile beaming with joy or not, it makes no difference to the brain. It moves the same facial muscles and sends the same signals to the brain, which produces happiness hormones. In this way, you can put yourself in a better and more optimistic mood, from which you can achieve better results and performance.

However, this also works the other way around, which is why to pay attention to your negative facial expressions. Running around with doubts on your face all the time makes them more and more solid in their own attitudes and impacting on all aspects of life.

If you want to use your facial expressions deliberately to improve your mood, we recommend the cozy atmosphere at your home. You may feel funny at first by the artificial smile, but the effect is worthwhile. In addition, such an applied smile in the facial expressions to other people is negative. If you do not really feel enjoy having fun, it's best to just smile for yourself - after that, the world usually looks very different.

FROM EMPATHY TO EMOTIONAL MANAGEMENT

CHAPTER TEN: Neuro Linguistic Programming and What Is Its Purpose?

Neuro linguistic programming (NLP) is a set of practical methods for changing the operation of one's mind and influencing other people. The system was based on the observation and analysis of the activities of experts in these fields - outstanding therapists, leaders, and businesspeople.

Neuro linguistic programming was developed in the mid-1970s in the United States by Richard Bandler and John Grinder. Researchers analyzed the issue of the effectiveness of the leading psychotherapists of that period - Fritz Perls, Virginia Satir, and Milton Erickson. They found that they make good contact with patients and initiate positive changes in their mental situation by using specific patterns of verbal and non-verbal communication. Based on their research, Bandler and Grinder have developed a series of simple and effective methods to change the way of thinking and acting that can be applied in various areas - personal development, interpersonal communication, in psychotherapy or business.

10.1 What is Neuro-Linguistic Programming?

The name "neuro-linguistic programming" (in short - NLP) refers to three domains integrated into this method. The "neuro" element deals with issues related to brain functioning, specifically cognitive processes - perception, thinking, remembering. The term "linguistic" refers to the relationship of the method with learning about the language understood as the basic communication tool, among other things - influencing other people. The concept of "programming" refers to how information is organized in learning processes. The "programs" created at that time are more or less effective ways of acting, tools for achieving life goals that people use to interact with reality. Neurolinguistics (in terms of NLP) is intended to change established mind programs to those that better serve the interests of the individual. Modification can relate to one's own behavior and feelings, but also to the way people think and act. NLP is, therefore, a kind of strategy for managing mental processes that affect attitudes and behavior. It can be a tool for self-development, support others in this process, and also serve as a method of persuasion.

10.2 NLP Techniques, Or Methods of Programming the Mind

The NLP method is based on creating conscious, active connections between thoughts and behaviors. Examples of these types of techniques are:

- **Anchoring** - a type of conditioning involving the combination of specific thoughts and feelings with selected stimuli, so that the desired emotional state can easily be induced at any time,

- **Modeling** - mapping the model of the behavior of people who have been successful in a particular field to develop the same characteristics and achievements,

- **Swish pattern** - getting rid of unwanted habits (e.g., compulsions) by replacing them with accepted ones, thanks to the visualization of a quick swap of images associated with these behaviors,

- **Rearranging** - a change in emotional states related to given circumstances by changing the way they are interpreted, i.e., giving positive meanings to events that were initially received as negative,

- **Timeline** - a change in the linear organization of thinking about past, present, and future events in a way that allows you to use the best mental resources on a regular basis.

NLP is also a series of techniques that can be used to influence other people. They are based on the appropriate use of verbal and non-verbal messages. Thanks to simple procedures, such as changing the word order or maintaining the right tone of the voice, effective communication is possible, which allows achieving the intended goals in interpersonal contacts. For example, starting a sentence with the phrase "imagine" causes the listener to open his mind to ideas that will be presented later in the speech, making it easier to recognize them as their own.

NLP in practice

Neuro-linguistic programming is based on the assumption that everyone has the resources they need to succeed. All he needs is the ability to use them. The right set of techniques allows you to optimize activities so that they begin to bring the desired results in areas such as, for example, learning knowledge, controlling anxiety, team management or seduction techniques. NLP can be used in business, management, sales, psychotherapy, coaching, education, treatment, and advocate practice. In each field, your own effectiveness is raised based on effective models, used - often unconsciously - by people who successfully achieve their goals.

The controversy around the NLP method

Scientific communities often criticize neuro linguistic programming because its effectiveness cannot be proven, i.e., the impact of NLP courses on the quality of life of participants can be estimated. The thin line between persuasion and manipulation, which is easily crossed in the framework of neuro-linguistic programming, also raises controversies. Opponents of the method point to the fact that it omits the ethical aspects of the proposed art of persuasion because techniques of conducting effective communication can easily be used to influence others against their will.

Notwithstanding the above opinions on NLP, its methods are of great interest, especially in areas such as advertising or commercial negotiations. NLP courses to increase self-motivation or communication skills are also popular.

CHAPTER ELEVEN: Benefit Of neuro-linguistic Programming (NLP)

1. Refined self-knowledge

Many times we do not know each other enough. It sounds strange to say that, but it's true. Self-awareness is such a current practice because of this demand for closer contact with our interiors.

The NLP is excellent for this type of question. The idea here is to promote self-awareness and then create an ideal mindset for personal development. It will depend on the professional area of application. However, almost all of them benefit from this kind of understanding.

It is only through the right strategies that you can get there. According to the customer response pattern, you will shape and transform it into something positive, staying closer to the end goal.

We live in an environment that very often leads us to live centered on the plane of exteriority. The ornamental stimuli of Christmas, the consumption of this time and the urgency to finish the pending projects before the end of the year are an example of how to look inside, and it is essential to increase introspection consciously.

2. Development of socio-emotional maturity

Sometimes personal development problems are linked to emotional and social maturity. This may be happening even in the workplace. Therefore, programming aims to work directly or indirectly with this issue.

As the terms already suggest, you need to achieve a development both in the way your emotions are processed and in the way you communicate and convey your feelings to others.

Facing even the most complicated of situations positively, strategically and intelligently is the shortest way to achieve autonomy and quality of life. You just need to start practicing to identify the advances.

3. Leadership mindset

Are you a business manager or owner of your own business? These are situations where the leadership mindset is mandatory. Some people are born predisposed to occupy this kind of position. The problem is that others are not mentally prepared.

Neuro-linguistic programming acts quickly and conveniently to achieve an effective leadership position. As there are values, traits, and behaviors that are very characteristic of a leadership figure, it is simpler to condition personal and professional performance.

You can become a good modern leader by utilizing the benefits of this strategy for years. The capacity for personal expression, mediation, and personal image are some of the fields that present advances.

4. Optimism and motivation in strategic analysis

Confidence and motivation are two of the most sought after traits when we are talking about setting up a positive mindset. It turns out that these are naturally subjective notions. What programming does is turn concepts into something technical.

Thus, we can work on exact customer behaviors to end frustration and demotivation, especially in the professional environment.

5. Overcoming limiting beliefs

Perhaps you have internalized limiting beliefs about yourself, about life, about love, about friendship, or about luck. Beliefs that are not an aim truth. However, the effect they produce on you is that of an immovable certainty. Because you have repeated these messages so often that you have become accustomed to them.

However, these limiting beliefs lead you to typecast yourself in a role that does not apply to you. They are premises that are closing doors for how they influence the level of emotion and action.

What is the positive side of these limiting beliefs? That you can renew this information from the internalization of new empowerment formulas that boost your growth from self-esteem. Through NLP you can find the key to these conscious statements that nourish your happiness.

6. Body language

It is impossible for a human being not to communicate information about himself. Through its presence in a place, even in the first impressions, it produces an image in the interlocutor. Communication not only takes the power of the word as a thread but also of body language.

The alignment between both areas is so important that to increase the effectiveness in the expression of a message, body communication must be in connection with the word. Otherwise, a form of noise is produced that conditions the understanding of the expressed.

Through NLP, you can increase your level of understanding of your body language by being able to reinforce this knowledge constructively in your relationships.

Quality communication is one of the most essential ingredients of social ties on a personal and professional level. When you improve your ties with others, you are happier.

7. Be your best version

No matter how old you are if you have the desire to evolve, you can do it. This capacity for learning that leads a human being to strengthen his brand through the pursuit of excellence is one of the benefits of NLP.

That is, you can not only observe yourself in your reality and your current circumstances; you can also observe your potential projection from the visualization of the person you want to become.

You can integrate this growth mindset into your life script because just as you can unlearn certain aspects, you can learn new ones.

You can be your best version by undertaking new learning, reinforce what makes you unique and move beyond the comfort zone where you feel comfortable to reach that desired horizon. Being your best version is a motivational stimulus. A mantra of overcoming.

8. Take the reins of your present

Preventing the past or external circumstances from being a limiting excuse in your happiness. NLP can help you lead your personal project as the protagonist of it through the search for your own excellence by increasing your level of self-confidence in yourself.

11.1How to Treat Anxiety Disorders With NLP

The anxiety disorders are, generally speaking, what mental health professionals use to describe a state of fear abnormal and pathological. Although there are many different types of anxiety disorders, including generalized anxiety disorder, phobic disorder, obsessive-compulsive disorder, social phobia, post-traumatic stress disorder, and panic disorder, the traditional treatment approach usually involves a combination of medications. And psychotherapy.

Anxiety disorders are a mental and emotional state (in the head) that is expressed in a variety of terms: palpitations, tremors, difficulty breathing, chest and abdominal pain, nausea, dizziness, agitation, fatigue, key-up, irritable sleep, difficulty and / or concentration, muscular tension, and extreme fear (of death, loss of control, and insanity).

In most cases, internal feelings are known as kinesthetic representations. This means that feelings of anxiety are senses (kinesthetic) internally in response to irrational thoughts and fears.

The anxiety is also known as racing thoughts syndrome. Its etymological origin comes from the Latin anxietas, anxious and anguere. These words mean, respectively, "anguish" and "anxiety", "disturbed" and "uncomfortable" and "squeeze" and "suffocate".

Produced by factors based on over- concern, anxiety causes tension, fears as well as physical symptoms with no real foundation. With a growing presence in humans, this is considered the "disease" of the century. It results, in effect, from the pressure and stress felt in everyday life.

Different Types of Anxiety

- **Panic Disorder:** May be characterized by frequent panic attacks. Those who suffer from this disorder are always afraid that crises may recur. This situation causes even more anxiety and emotional instability.

- **Generalized Anxiety:** It is characterized by excessive worry, in everyday life, with no apparent cause.

- **Obsessive-Compulsive Disorder:** These are unwelcome behaviors or impulses that trigger anxiety and end up being persistent. For example, the individual is unable to control himself over a simple hand wash. Do widespread cleaning all the time, need to feel absolute control over situations and make exhaustive counts.

- **Posttraumatic stress:** These are experienced events that eventually resurface. Constantly reliving these traumatic events in the present through images, words or thoughts generates increased emotional instability. Thus, it leads to insomnia, irritability, lack of concentration, among other symptoms.

- **Phobias:** The individual feels an exaggerated fear of an object, an animal or a particular situation. However, the anxiety felt is excessive in relation to the real danger that this experience or exposure represents at that particular moment.

Anxiety symptoms

Physicists:

- Shortness of breath and chest tightness;

- Muscle tensions;

- Insomnia;

- Irritability;

- Difficulty breathing as well as a lump in the throat;

- Spasms.

Psychological:

- Nervousness;

- Agoraphobia;

- Constant fear;

- Exaggerated concerns and uncontrolled thoughts;

- Lack of concentration.

Anxiety results from our own cognitive distortions.

We live in a world of assumptions and few goals. But these assumptions turn out to be uncertainties and dubious events.

Despite the potential to generate hope or fear, happiness, or pain, they can lead to hallucinations, tiredness, and weariness.

This is a continuous and active self-hypnotic procedure that can have health benefits. By anticipating future challenges and goals, we can appreciate their importance and also realize our ability to respond.

In a healthy person, fear is a realistic assessment of the severity of the challenge. It is also able to mobilize the body to cope with it. Through increased pulse and breathing, the muscles are eventually stimulated. On the contrary, in a person suffering from anxiety, certain cognitive distortions occur.

Through NLP and Hypnosis, it is possible to work on these same sub modalities and the subconscious. Sometimes a resignification of the vision, hearing, and sensation that the person may have is made.

How to treat anxiety with NLP and Hypnosis?

Anxiety sufferers who contact me (me or another therapist) seek advice and support above all. The goal is to put into action a plan that will change your life. Although we do not have a magic wand to solve the problem, we were able to make significant changes. For this to happen, we need to do what we suggest and be open to the experience.

With Neuro-linguistic Programming (NLP), we explain to the client how the brain works. Thus, we help reverse the cognitive distortions that lead you to certain anxiety situations. This is done through resignification of symptoms, alteration of submodalities, resources/solutions, and teaching the application of trance and relaxation anchors.

With hypnosis, we try to discover the source of anxiety and to understand what caused the symptoms. Through some techniques, it is possible to apply triggers to your unconscious and thus redirect it into tasks, words, and attitudes.

This will not only slow down the brain but also improve neurotransmitter balance (e.g., serotonin, dopamine, or norepinephrine). They will serve as fuels for the brain to perform certain functions.

11.2Other Tools for Reducing Anxiety Disorders Treatment.

The Timelines

Each person has a peculiar way of coding time. The past, present, and future are organized in each person in such a way that, when accessing memory, you can know which is which and at what time it moves.

Working with the Timeline gives a completely different understanding of time, based on an understanding of how the brain works.

The Framing

Framing is an NLP technique that involves the use of language patterns to "rethink" the perceptual distortions characteristic of anxiety disorders. Nothing that exists in this world makes sense by itself. People assign meanings according to their beliefs, values, likes and dislikes, and other concerns. The meaning of an experience and therefore is dependent on the context of the experience.

Framing is a strategy that works to change the way someone perceives an event and change the meaning it has given to that event. When the meaning changes, the response, and behavior also changes.

Alter submodalities

In NLP, submodalities are the specific characteristics of internal representations. For example, we have already mentioned visual form and one of internal representation. Visual images have distinctive features, such as black and white in front, near or far, you look in the image or are looking through your own eyes, the size of the image and bright or matte. Changing the submodalities of experience can reduce the emotional intensity of that experience.

Parts Integration

Answers of anxiety and panic are inconsistent with the rest of a person's life. It is as if the part of the person who is in control at the time of panic or anxiety crisis has its own intentions, beliefs, and behaviors that are different from the intentions, beliefs, and behaviors of the same person when he is calm. There are numerous NLP techniques that are useful for the integration of beliefs and parties to create congruence between the person's thoughts and feelings and the elimination of irrational thoughts and feelings that generate anxiety.

Our mind is powerful. Just as it can make fear, nervousness, and anxiety unmanageable, it can also be used positively. The strength you have to have a destructive effect on your life can be used to overcome problems.

In this sense, there are some tips you can follow to combat anxiety: Stop, rest, divide tasks, do not exert pressure, communicate, meditate, and read. These suggestions can be referred to as anxiety cleansing treatment. In addition, they serve to prevent other problems that arise from this: phobias and panic, as well as depression. Take care of your being!

11.3 Stress Management and NLP

Stress is a psycho physical response that the individual puts in place in dealing with certain situations in life. Stress is not necessarily negative, but in those cases where the situations to be addressed exceed personal and social resources; we enter a pathological state that involves the exhaustion of the body's energies, affecting mental, and physical balance.

The accumulation of stress becomes an unpleasant sensation during the workday. The worker has the feeling of going against the clock most of the time instead of proactively managing the tasks. Stress adds fatigue to one's work in the office. In the final stretch of the year, there are many professionals who take stock of their employment situation to make adjustments, changes, and modifications in their routine to increase well-being.

Different types of stress

What defines a stressful situation? Although it is not possible to define it a priori, if we do not take into consideration the individual characteristics of the person facing a situation, we can identify different categories of stress: a chronic environmental stress due to situations that recur over time with a certain frequency , an acute stress due to a critical event.

1. Chronic environmental stress

This Concerns situations that are part of an individual's lifestyle, such as an unsatisfactory quality of sleep or limited autonomy in the organization of their work. These situations are not stressful if they occur sporadically but become so when they become chronic in people's life habits, and for this reason, their gravity is often underestimated.

2. Acute stress due to a critical event

It concerns any situation that leads people to experience particularly strong emotional reactions, such as to interfere with their ability to act both at the time of the event and later. Critical events can, for example, be serious accidents in which there is a danger of life, police shootings, sudden layoffs at work. In these situations, the ability to emotionally process the situation is put into crisis.

3. The stress of emergency professionals

There are professional categories, such as the military in war scenarios or health workers in emergency departments, who frequently confront critical events that become part of their working day. In these situations, if the staff is not adequately supported, in addition to high levels of stress, it is high the probability in these people of developing emotional exhaustion and an attitude of cynicism towards others.

11.4 Managing stress through NLP

- Imagine a situation in your professional life in which you felt fully happy and fulfilled. Close your eyes take a deep breath and try to recreate yourself in the sensations of that moment (sensations that come to your presence through this recreation). Project your strengths from that moment in situations that currently cause you stress and that you want to overcome: What do you admire about yourself at that time and what can you do to bring up these capacities that are in you?

- At least three days a week, do the exercise of saying goodbye to the day by writing down in your diary three daily moments in which you have felt good about yourself. What factors have depended on you at that time? List a list of these aspects to increase your resources in situations that cause you stress.

- When we feel stress, we can use avoidance as a defense mechanism so as not to cope with that discomfort we feel when we are in emotional tension. In this way, fear of fear occurs. The most important thing to reduce stress at work is to stay on the move, that is, to seek the rest that gives us in certain moments the security of being in the comfort zone but leaving at many other times towards the learning zone. Leaving the comfort zone and practical experience is vital to train personal resources in the face of stress. No matter how many people we have, this potential is reduced if we do not put our resources into practice.

- Analyze what your world map is and how you relate to the environment: Do you perceive the environment as an external threat? So, the logical response to this threat is the position of defense and stress can be a mechanism. Therefore, to change your emotional state and increase your inner peace of mind you must rethink your position in your company and how you can change the perspective. Think of a co-worker whom you admire for his charisma, a person who conveys confidence and self-confidence: What can you do to model these attitudes?

- When the stress continues overtime beyond the specific event that caused it, it is essential that you try to identify the recurring images that come to your mind accompanied by sensations and ideas that do not make you feel good. To consciously modify these sensations through the memory of other moments in which you have had opposite perceptions of well-being is an excellent way to break this dynamic of emotional stress.

- People suffer more stress from the interpretation we make of the facts than from the reality itself. In these types of cases, it is recommended that you ask yourself this question: What beliefs are altering your interpretation of reality so you consider that fact that worries you a problem that affects your well-being? Write those beliefs in writing and most likely, when you can visualize them, you realize that your reality changes at the moment you change. And this approach which is so important is the one that most often costs those who position themselves as mere victims of a difficult context. You can use the phrase.

- State your intention to stop feeling stressed positively. For example, you can mark this premise: "I want to feel calm at work." You can also do the exercise of writing a story using metaphors that help you find inspiration in that story. To do this, you can write it thinking that later you will send it to a friend who is suffering from stress: What story could you tell to help you change your perspective?

- The body also communicates stress through its language. It is important that when you are going to face a situation that involves extra effort on an emotional level, pay attention to the language of your body to adopt a correct posture. Try to walk with your back straight and look straight ahead.

- Do not feel stress about failures since there are no professional defeats but the feedback of reality that gives you the necessary information for your personal development.

- NLP has a lot to do with language and linguistics. From this perspective, some words are especially conducive to generating stress. One of them is "I have to." From now on, try modifying your inner dialogue to change this expression to the formula "I want." While the first option produces the feeling of the weight of an obligation, on the contrary, the message "I want" conveys the conviction of a decision.

- Participating in an NLP course in a coaching school is a vital learning measure to acquire new resources. Some people are very demanding of themselves, and behind the stress, there can also be large doses of guilt. It is recommended that if you feel stressed, you think that you have acted the best you have known at all times.

Other tools on how to manage stress

Stress, is a multidimensional phenomenon, must be addressed by considering multiple levels: the physiology of the organism, the emotional states, and thoughts of the individual and his significant social relationships. In these levels, it will be necessary to improve the resources that the person can use to cope with stress.

1. The physiology of the organism

We all have a representation of the body within our brain, a sort of topographical image that allows us to experience our physicality; despite this, everyone has a different experience of his muscular districts. So they are possible stress management different relationships with one's body, and this also implies a different capacity to monitor it through sensations. Stress influences the body's physiology through hormone production, if these changes are underestimated or ignored the bodies energies soon will be exhausted, or a prolonged hyper-activation could favor pathological phenomena (such as cardiovascular events). A relevant aspect of stress management is to improve the relationship with one's body and its sensations.

2. Emotions

Stress also affects mood. Furthermore, the mood that a person has in the base may or may not predispose one to face situations, such as those with underlying anxiety will tend to experience unforeseen events as catastrophic events more easily. Emotional information can be processed by the brain either in a more instinctual way or in a more reasoned way (for a more extensive discussion of the processing of emotional information in the brain, see the article "Paths of Emotions ". A frequent processing instinctual subjects the organism to a greater reactivity to the situations that occur to the individual; therefore it becomes important to facilitate a greater modulation of the emotional states through more reasoned processing.

3. Thoughts

When faced with a situation perceived as stressful, it is essential to consider what the person's cognitive approach is, for example, if it is believed that it is possible to face the situation or prefer to avoid it. A better approach does not exist a priori, and it depends both on the characteristics of the situation and above all, on the individual's ability to have flexible mental approaches. In this case, we can work to improve the ability to solve problems and produce more solution alternatives.

4. Relationship with others

We have known for several years that there are not only individual resources and capacities but also social ones, or how important effective persons can provide emotional support. Although this is a concrete aspect that depends on the significant people of our lives, we must consider that every individual during his existence implements relational strategies to build deep and lasting relationships. These strategies may be more or less effective, or even trespassing into a social inhibition in which one's emotional states rarely manifest themselves to others for fear of being rejected. Working on relational skills is another important element of a multidimensional stress approach.

CHAPTER TWELVE: Panic Attack

A panic attack is a short episode of anxiety that has no specific cause or can be triggered by a stressful situation. The patient is afraid that he will die, faint, or lose control. Check out what to know about panic attacks and how to deal with them.

Each of us has experienced fear for their lives at least once in our lives. Usually, when we are afraid, we have rational reasons for this. A panic attack is different. It can reach us everywhere - at home, at work, in the elevator, behind the wheel.

Feeling fear is a natural thing in an emergency. Breath and pulse are accelerated, muscles tighten. Anxiety in the event of a panic attack is irrational. It comes suddenly, cannot be predicted and gradually increases. It can appear without any cause perceptible to the patient, related to a specific situation that causes anxiety or is caused by a disease. If you have experienced such a condition once, you will certainly not mistake it for any other.

Symptom

Panic attacks usually begin suddenly, without warning. They can appear at any time: when you are driving, in a mall, when you are sound asleep or in the middle of a business meeting. You may have occasional or frequent panic attacks.

A person who experiences a panic attack feels very sick. He has the impression that he will soon die or lose control. He can cry and call an ambulance. Some people are afraid of having a heart attack. There is a feeling of unrealness and disconnection from your own body. Characteristic is the fear of subsequent attacks, the so-called fear of fear.

A panic attack can last from a few to several minutes to an hour.

Panic attacks have many variants, but the symptoms usually peak in minutes. After the panic attack disappears, you may feel fatigued and exhausted.

Panic attacks usually include any of these signs or symptoms:

- The feeling of danger or impending doom
- Fear of losing control or death
- Tachycardia and palpitations
- Sweat
- Tremors or shaking
- Shortness of breath or tightness in the throat
- Shaking chills
- Hot flushes
- Sickness
- Abdominal cramps
- Chest pain
- Headache
- Dizziness, lightheadedness or fainting
- Feeling numb or tingling
- Feelings of unreality or disconnection

One of the worst aspects of panic attacks is the intense fear of recurrence. That fear can be so strong that it can make you avoid certain situations in which they could occur.

Panic attack - causes

Panic attacks occur in 9% of the population. Women get sick twice as often as men. The causes of panic attacks are not entirely known. They can occur in people with the following mental disorders:

- panic disorder

- generalized anxiety disorder (anxiety neurosis),

- anxiety disorder in the form of phobia (agoraphobia, social phobia),

- affective disorders (depression),

- reaction to severe stress or adaptive disorders,

- psychotic disorders (see - psychosis).

Symptoms of panic attacks can also occur in such somatic diseases as:

- paroxysmal hypoglycemia

- pheochromocytoma,

- mitral valve prolapse,

- tetany,

- acute ischemic heart disease,

- Epilepsy.

Panic attacks also occur in healthy people in stressful situations.

12.1 Effective Breathing Techniques to Reduce Anxiety

Breathing techniques remind us that this metabolic act is much more than a physical process. Breathing well produces pleasure, relieves anxiety, and allows us to live better. It would, therefore, be beneficial to make breathing a much more conscious, focused, and harmonious act in our daily lives.

Most people never stop to analyze the way they breathe. The question would be, why do it? Our organism is a perfect machine that performs many processes automatically, ensuring our survival. Thanks to this, we can devote much of our energy to other tasks, such as reading this article, for example.

As I breathe, I see myself as a water mirror. As I exhale, I reflect on things as they are."

- Thich Nhat Hanh –

Reflecting on all this can do us great. Neglecting the body and allowing our emotions to dominate us has serious consequences. We must not forget that an exhausted organism, dominated or controlled by excessive worry, haste or anxiety translates into faster and more abnormal breathing, a body that performs its metabolic functions in an unbalanced and even dangerous way.

You need to breathe well to live better, and these techniques can help us.

1. Breathing Techniques: Diaphragmatic Breathing

When we think of breathing, we instantly visualize a pair of lungs. Well, we can say that the real responsible for this process is the diaphragm. It is located below the lungs and separates the chest from the abdominal area. It moves when we breathe, and if we do it broadly, we will stimulate other organs such as the liver and a large amount of tissue to promote blood circulation and even the elimination of toxins.

We should pay attention to this area of our body because the diaphragm is an essential part of most breathing techniques. Let's look at how to become aware of it and how to stimulate it.

- Place one hand on the abdomen and the other on the chest.

- The shoulders should be erect.

- Now breathe deeply through your nose.

- Bring air to the diaphragm (abdomen), not to the chest.

- Exhale through your mouth in a sonorous way.

- Ideally, take between 6 or 10 slow breaths per minute.

2. Alternate Nose Breathing

This is one of the best-known breathing techniques. It is also ideal for reducing anxiety, relaxing, and promoting better concentration in everyday life. We should follow these steps:

- Sit comfortably with your spine straight.

- Now, with the right thumb, press the right nostril.

- Then breathe in deeply through the left nostril to the ceiling.

- Hold your breath and then press the left nostril and exhale from the right.

- Repeat the process in reverse.

It may seem complicated at first, but as soon as we automate the steps, we will feel their benefits.

3. The breath of the shiny skull or kapalabhati

Kapalabhati is one of the most curious and effective breathing techniques to reduce anxiety and optimize our respiratory system. It helps us clear the airways and even improves lung capacity.

The term kapalabhati comes from Sanskrit and is composed of two concepts: kapala, which means "skull" and bhati, which means "brightness or cleansing." Let's see what it consists of:

- Sit with your back straight.

- Bring your chin to your chest.

- Close your eyes to focus better on breathing.

- Breathe in deeply.

- Now do: Make rapid exhales by contracting the muscles in your abdomen, imagining that you are touching your navel to your spine.

- As you exhale, your body will inhale automatically. Ideally, do it at least 10 to 15 times in a row. Rest a few minutes and start over.

Briefly, this technique consists of slow, deep breaths followed by rapid and forceful exhalation.

4. Visualization Breathing Technique

Many breathing techniques include multiple visualizations to achieve deeper relaxation. However, it takes a little more experience for the whole process to benefit us and give us cathartic sensations that can ease tensions and reduce anxiety or stress.

So note this very original strategy.

- Lie on the floor on a mat or even on the bed.

- Place one hand on your abdomen and one on your chest to make sure you are breathing through the diaphragm.

- Take a deep breath through your nose, imagine that you are on a beach and a wave is warmly covering you from feet to the head. Feel its freshness, the bubbling water, the smell of the sea.

- Exhale through your mouth and visualize the same wave receding slowly, relaxingly…

These simple breathing techniques can help us improve our well-being, take care of our health, and untie all the tensions that almost unknowingly make us sick. Let's find a few minutes throughout the day to breathe better, to live in harmony with our own body and its needs.

CHAPTER THIRTEEN: Step Plan to Turn Weaknesses into Strengths

Research shows that 97% of people can easily identify a limiting habit of their professional careers. We are unreliable, lack empathy, avoid conflict, or fear risk. Although we are clear that our weaknesses cost us personally and professionally, few of us make any progress in turning them into strengths. In fact, managers' report that after giving feedback to subordinates in the performance review, less than 10% chance for the following year. It does not have to be this way.

The keys to improving most of the weaknesses are:

Identify crucial moments: Bad habits and chronic weaknesses are usually not for a simple cognitive or behavioral gap in our abilities but to a deeply habitual and practiced response to feelings of anxiety, ineptitude, or fear. The way forward is to identify the nature of the moments that cause those ineffective responses. Pay attention to the moments, places, social circumstances, moods, psychological states, or perception of risks that encourage you to act in ways that lead to poor results. These are your crucial moments. The good news about the crucial moments is that they reduce the size of your problem. The change seems overwhelming when you think it requires permanent vigilance. In fact, it's usually just about driving a few minutes a day better than before.

Designing deliberate practices: Swedish researcher Anders Ericsson has shown that our learning curves speed up when we fall into what he described as deliberate practice. These are little episodes of intense focus, where we practice a skill under relatively real conditions. If these intense episodes of practice are accompanied with immediate feedback, learning speeds up even more. The psychologist Albert Bandura refers to this as guided mastery and discovered that we can overcome deep emotional barriers if we conduct this skills test under circumstances with the right mix of safety and challenge.

Once you know your crucial moments, identify moderately challenging situations where you can practice the aim skill. An important element of deliberate practice is the focus on individual skill. If you are studying skills for crucial conversations, focus on one: for example, creating security.

Develop emotional competence: Ensure that your plan includes the development of skills to handle the inevitable emotions that accompany the confrontation with a weakness. Simply forcing yourself to try terrifying or uncomfortable behavior is not a success in itself; provoking those unpleasant emotions will simply reinforce that this is an act to avoid. You should look for tactics that you can use to make unpleasant action more pleasant or at least manageable. By doing so, you gradually retrain your brain to change the formula with which you predict how you will feel in your crucial moments.

You can change the habit that limits your career by identifying your own crucial moments, looking for brief and intentional opportunities to deliberately practice and building skills to deal with the emotional barriers that limit your progress. Do not let fear or inertia hold you back.

Other ways to Transform Your Weaknesses into Strengths

Unfortunately, most of us give importance and praise only our strengths and qualities, and we forget to analyze what is not good for our weaknesses. This is everything in life, both personal and professional.

In business life, it is essential that we do a market analysis, and this analysis encompasses the study of weaknesses because that is where the greatest opportunities lie. A successful business knows how to analyze the market and self-analyze to turn weaknesses into opportunities.

When we are entrepreneurs it is essential that we have this broad vision; It is necessary to look down and realize what is not working, accept our shortcomings, and realize that we need people to perform functions that we are not good at; From the moment our perceptions change, we can better seize opportunities and make good choices.

Our life is made up of several areas, and all of them are connected — physical, mental, social, spiritual, and professional state. We need to be aware of all areas of our lives and work, especially on those that are not doing as well as we would like. Remember, when we have an area that is becoming a weak point, it ends up affecting the other areas and causing numerous problems and dissatisfaction.

Whether you are an entrepreneur or not, a tip for life is: Be smart and work out your weaknesses into strongholds. Improve the living areas that you understand as weaknesses in two simple steps:

1 - Self-knowledge: We must know ourselves as nobody. Do a self-analysis, a list of your strengths and weaknesses, study all these points? Find your qualities and shortcomings. Understand which areas of your life are not making you happy, and ask yourself why. Know what your purpose is, and how to define how its characteristics will help you achieve this purpose. List, write, it is important that it is clear to you and that it helps you to accept all its characteristics, both good and bad. From this moment on your perception of yourself will be well defined, so you will know what needs to be improved and what can be turned into opportunities and strengths.

2 - Planning / Actions: By getting self-knowledge, everything will be clearer and more transparent to you; self-knowledge will bring you much wisdom. With this, you will surely be more motivated and aiming to bring improvements to your life. If you have recognized that the physical area is not as it should be, it is clear that you should take actions such as going to the doctor, checking up, eating properly, and doing physical activities; This is taking actions to have new healthy habits, for example.

It is a process, first analysis, the recognition of the problem, with that comes wisdom, and from there you must strategize and take action to solve. For this to really take shape, after self-awareness you need to set your goals, plan to reach them and do what you have to do. Some tools help with this process and even motivate you to follow your planning.

A powerful tool is planners! I am adept at this tool because I know the power of writing goals and having daily noted what should be done. I changed my life from the moment I started writing my goals because I can set my tasks and organize my whole day.

3- Identify them: The first step in converting a weakness into a strength is to identify those weaknesses. It exercises maturity and strength to sit and think about what things in your life really represent a weak part of you, but if you don't do this first, then it will be impossible to improve.

4- Accept them: There is nothing wrong with you accepting the weaknesses you may have. We all find it hard to assume that we may have defects or weaknesses, but once we understand that we have them and accept them as part of our personality we can begin the process to improve.

5- Understand its origin: All our weaknesses or defects have an origin, come from some part of our upbringing or our personality. To improve these weaknesses and strengthen them, it is necessary to understand where they come from. This way you can also understand what aspect of your personality you should improve.

6- Set goals: The only way to improve an aspect of our personality is to set a goal to do so. Therefore, if you really want that weakness to become a strength, the first step is to know what steps you should take to do it, once you know, stay attached to the plan and monitor your progress.

There is no other way to improve and change a weakness for strength is not with effort and dedication. It is entirely workable to achieve it if you accept that weakness, understand where it comes from and then set the goal of improving it.

CHAPTER FOURTEEN: The Reality of Life in Conversation

We all try to know what are the truths of the world in which we live. We dedicate great material and intellectual efforts to apprehend the reality of things. We look for a certain sense of security that allows us to continue looking forward with confidence.

We also know that we quite cannot foresee the future and that the essential things in life, despite the advances of our scientific knowledge, are a matter of beliefs or faith given the impossibility of their understanding of what which are (God, death, meaning ...). As Wittgenstein would say, they are outside the limits of our world; they are transcendental. Fortunately, there is a place for mysticism in our lives since a mystery surrounds us to which, perhaps, our most coherent attitude should be silence: what we cannot talk about must be silenced.

But this does not mean that we cannot aspire to a richer and fuller life. We must believe in life and the possibilities of progress (not just material) that are open to us. If we choose i, we can live in a livable and comforting world. In this belief of free will (whether true or not) and our ability to choose, is where our true essence lies as beings with the conscience that we are. In our life happening, in our daily social and pragmatic practice, it is where we can and should talk.

Loud and clear through our choices and character. What we know, and consequently, how we act, is a matter of conversation and social practice that depends on us and our relationship with others. There is nothing in the deepest part of us that we have not put there ourselves.

And sometimes the only way forward is not making us the more rigorous but being more imaginative by crossing limits, most times, self-imposed: feel the mystery and shut up and then confidently speak and act. Life is, therefore, a matter of Faith: in ourselves and others. No great demonstrations are needed, If we can trust others, we no longer need to believe anything else, and that is certainly fortunately in our hand through the discourse that we consciously choose from our lives.

14.1 The art of conversation: How to connect with people?

Effective conversation should be based on three basic keys: listening, empathy and connection.

We all know how to maintain a dialogue, but are we effective in carrying out a quality conversation? Oddly enough, the answer is often "no." Not everyone dominates the art of conversational intelligence, that with which to authentically connect with someone exchanging information effectively.

Talking is also creating an impact. It is not enough just to "like". Sometimes, that is not even what we are looking for; What we want is for our message to arrive, for us to be credible and for us to establish a fluid and direct connection with the interlocutor. Now, something we see and experience frequently is dialogues in which there is someone who does not listen and who, at times, comes to use violent communication.

Ismael Cala, one of the best exponents in the field of personal development, often reminds us that all effective communication must start from Emotional Intelligence. With regard to the art of conversation, the same thing happens; People must learn to manage emotions, to apply empathy and to use assertiveness properly.

Learning to communicate and have a conversation says a lot about us. It is our gateway to meet people, to improve our work and even to reach agreements and solve problems.

The conversation: the art of connecting from emotions and respect

Winston Churchill said, with great success, that a good conversation should exhaust the issues, not the interlocutors. Thus, it is common that sometimes we give someone who instead of talking establishes monologues. Other people, on the other hand, limit themselves to being condescending, to reaffirm each comment without enriching the dialogue with their contributions.

That this happens means that it is necessary to work various aspects of our psychological fabric. Sometimes, insecurity makes us afraid to give our opinion. Other times, we lack those skills that allow us to make use of real empathy with which to read between the lines and understand certain clues of the other person's nonverbal language.

That is why in these cases, it is useful to keep in mind some simple tips that allow us to reflect:

Pause, empathy, needs: the PEN strategy

To master the art of conversation, it will be very good for us to internalize the word PEN. This term integrates three key dimensions:

Pause. It is that interval of time that we must pass before responding to a person when we have a dialogue. These seconds of silence will allow us to meditate better what we are going to say.

Empathy. Likewise, as we have indicated previously, being able to understand and empathize with the emotional reality of the other will undoubtedly help us to take care of the quality of the dialogue much more.

Needs During a conversation, we should never let go of our needs. It is clear that we will always respect the other, but it is necessary not to stay in the background, not to be overwhelmed or manipulated. A dialogue must be dynamic; This way, we will always avoid protecting ourselves from violent communication.

Watch the tone

Some people speak too loudly, annoyingly, or annoyingly. They are profiles whose voice, without saying anything aggressive, already puts us on the defensive. The classic phrase "it is not what you say but how you say it" gives us a clue of that aspect that we must control to the maximum in a conversation.

Own anecdotes account to build trust

We all like anecdotes. We like to be explained personal aspects because it is a way to give confidence. This infallible strategy is used in every successful conversation: telling anecdotes, telling experiences or events from the past ... It's a great way to break the ice and offer closeness.

Listen and show curiosity

Active listening is that psychic tendon that gives life to every good conversation. To perceive that our interlocutor is aware of us, that he listens to us carefully, that he knows how to read in every gesture, word, and detail generate comfort and confidence.

It is also very successful that we show curiosity, that we ask questions without falling into an interrogation or that we show genuine interest in knowing more about who we have in front of us.

To conclude, something that experts in the field of communication point out to us is that our big mistake in communicating is that we have stopped listening. Sometimes, we are more aware of other things: our own thoughts, the mobile, what happens around ... All of them are red flags that reduce the quality of the conversation.

14.2How to master the art of conversation

Forget the 10% inspiration, and there is 90% perspiration that ensures you will learn and master this art. Count on the 10% just to brighten the moment and not as a crutch. After all, no great artist lives on inspiration.

1 Mastering Body Language

Perhaps one of the oldest and most successful tips is to use body language to your advantage. After all, your body speaks, so it is better that it also makes a beautiful speech.

And some simple tips still seem to have a lot of effects. Always keep your feet on the floor, lean nowhere and rest, this "balance" transpires to the audience and gives them confidence.

Move onstage sparingly, don't be hurrying to and fro, be on time. Move from one place to another to dominate the space, or move towards the audience when telling something more intimate or some different detail. As if telling a secret.

Train in front of a mirror and see if your expressions match what you are talking about.

2 Tailor speeches to your listener

It is no use giving a talk to a group of farmworkers and creating a pompous speech as if you were speaking to senior executives. And that goes for everything from meetings to speeches to day-to-day chat.

Understand your audience, try to find out who they are and use their language. Approach them. Remember that the more you can be clear to them, the easier they absorb the information.

It is important that they feel that it was made to listen and it is not just any repetition. They need to feel unique.

3 Have authority on what you are talking about

It sounds crazy to have to say that, but it isn't. It's no use pretending if you're going to talk about something, study hard about it. And the more you study and know what you're talking about, the easier it is to master the art of speaking.

Simple, as you will have confidence in what you are talking about. It will not slip and will not be misled by doubt. So keep in mind, to master the art of speaking, the first step is to know well what you are talking about.

4 Good vocabulary and pronunciation

And here two tips in one. The first is to have a vocabulary developed, the more words and phrases you have in your repertoire and the easier it is to express what you mean clearly and effectively.

But do not confuse this with using difficult words to show that you have read the dictionary, but have different outputs for similar ideas and resources for not repeating ideas and expressions.

And the more you have this content at hand, the, more importantly; you'll be able to say it safely. Speak the whole words, with all "Rs" and "Is," without forgetting the "Ss" in plurals. Maintain an intense pace and speed that allows everyone to understand every word.

5 Listen to your audience

This tip, directly, is not so much for lectures and speeches, but is important for everyday life, whether in the office or at home. Listen to what people have to say, learn from each word; don't rush, and don't interrupt.

Listening to people makes them comfortable and makes them listen to you better after that. In lectures, one way to do this is by opening spaces for the audience to speak.

6 Find Your Own Personality

It's no use looking at that speaker you think is amazing and wanting to copy it. Use inspiration and reference, but go your own way. The more comfortable with yourself, the more your audience becomes comfortable with you.

Make mistakes, correct, go back and cut, when you see, you will realize that you are no longer a persona there talking to your audience, but yourself. Your true self. And there is no one better for you to be than yourself.

7 Whenever Possible, Tell Stories

Forget that modern concept of storytelling and storytelling. This works, but it's just another term for things that already existed. What matters here is that you're comfortable with your script, not letting it seem to jump from place to place without meaning.

It must have a beginning, middle, and end. Create a timeline where your talk follows accurately. Introduce the subject, develop it, defend an opinion, and pass some content, in the end, reaffirm everything you said and conclude.

CHAPTER FIFTEEN: Habits and Its Effect on Living

The habit is any behavior learned (not innate, not born with any habit) by repetition, which is performed regularly and automatically without hardly thinking about it. It is a basic element of human learning. According to scientists, habits, whether positive or harmful, are created because the brain always looks for ways to save effort, tries to modify any routine in a habit to save time and energy. This has the benefit that an efficient brain does not need so much space, so the head is smaller and childbirth easier. Also, by automating certain behaviors, its performance is fast and accurate, and by not having to concentrate on how to walk, breathe or eat, we can devote more time and energy to other things like experimenting and inventing. If the organism had to respond to all the amount of stimuli that occur in any situation, the behavior would be chaotic, so that the habituation has an evolutionary value by contributing to the adaptability of the organism, which response to the stimuli that for it are more relevant.

Changing habits is hard work, especially thinking habits. The thoughts we frequent every day on any issue become our natural way of thinking, because it demands much less effort for the brain always to think the same about the same issue already learned. At the beginning we must become aware of the necessary effort involved in having to concentrate on restructuring our negative automatic thoughts, but knowing that if we do it often and constantly (without allowing ourselves any exceptions) our neurons begin to interact with each other, creating more dynamic synaptic connections and intertwined in our brain to prepare our mind to assimilate what we have worked intellectually. Thus this new state of mind is transmitted to our consciousness. When we have the firm decision that the time has come to change our thinking,

Human beings have the power to renew ourselves, and we have the potential and the ability to transform ourselves into the person to whom we aspire mentally, consciously using the same tools with which we unconsciously elaborate our old Self. These characteristic of the human being are mental tools force of repetition, activation of new synapses by studying new knowledge or living new experiences, mindfulness in our environment (mindfulness) that allows us to interrupt the thoughts of recurrent concern, or also, on the contrary, to learn to realize from our dependence on the emotional state we have created. We must internalize that human beings are a process in constant transformation, we are a flow of experiences that enrich our perception of the world, and we often think of ways to improve our physical and social skills, and to change our behavior with close people. We can transform our automatic thoughts with determination, every day, to create new, more positive habits for us and thus renew our emotions and behaviors.

15.1 How Are Habits Formed

Habits are formed because of the brain changes in response to regular practice.

As we progress each day through acquiring knowledge, performing new tasks, and participating in informative conversations, our brains evolve and reprogram themselves to integrate these experiences. - Shawn Achor

Neuroscientists are used to saying that "neurons that light together work together". This means that there are billions of interconnected neurons in our brains that form a complex set of neural pathways. An electric current flows through these circuits, from neuron to neuron, sending messages that constitute each of our actions and thoughts. The more we perform a particular action, the more connections between the corresponding neurons. The stronger the link, the faster the message travels the circuit. This is what makes a behavior a second nature or an automatism.

15.2 How to Loose Bad Habits

Habits are behaviors in which we engage routinely and repeatedly, without which it would be very difficult to perform many of the tasks we do daily. In fact, if we are efficient in performing complex tasks, it is because we learned and internalized them, which allows us to do them without thinking. However, some become bad habits. Speaking, walking, writing, driving, or playing an instrument, for example, are some skills that are now rooted in our system.

Our brain does not have to think to execute them, so we are able to perform them routinely, without conscious effort. Therefore, we can conclude that habits are very useful for us. However, there are habits that we have formed that are not so productive and that are considered bad.

It is the case of the custom of biting the nails, facial tics, or uncontrolled movement of the feet while waiting, for example. These habits can be very annoying and unpleasant for others in social situations.

Habits such as scolding, criticizing, seeking attention in others or manipulation can also be considered annoying.

As with the habits that help us positively in our daily tasks, we also get involved in these negative activities without making any conscious effort; which, instead of helping us, can turn against us. Therefore, it is important to break these bad habits to improve interpersonal connections, social labels, and personal growth.

How to eliminate bad habits? Step by Step

Habits are behaviors learned based on extreme dedication, persistence, and awareness. The more we get involved in our habits, the more they take root and are reinforced in our system. However, every time we try to do something different from what our habits are, they tend to weaken and the new alternative behavior gradually strengthens with repeated use.

A breaking habit implies a step-by-step approach. Gillian Butler propose a six-step system to break bad habits. They are the following:

- Decide to change.

- Be aware of all the details related to those bad habits.

- Design strategies to help stop the habit.

- Replace the habit with alternative behavior.

- It persists in being consistent and tracking progress.

- Learn to manage lapses.

a) Decide to change

The first and most important thing to break a bad habit is to decide to get rid of that bad habit. When you think about the disadvantages of that habit, it is easier to make this decision. Just as important is thinking about the benefits that will come later.

But it is very difficult to cut a bad habit at the root just by deciding.

There are many people only with this step can, but it is not usual. If you are in the majority group, do not despair. You will get it if you make the decision and follow this program. So don't stop reading; you have 5 more steps left...

b) Be aware of all the details related to that bad habit

To stop a bad habit, you have to be aware that you have and that only you are able to eliminate it. It is also important to understand what that habit is that you want to eliminate and how it works.

You have to ask yourself why, under what circumstances, how ... and anything else that can help you make a detailed description of that bad habit. The fundamental point is to know what the environmental triggers that cause it are.

c) Design strategies to help stop the habit

With all the information collected in the previous step, you can now be aware and know when you are more likely to develop that bad habit before it happens. It is time to design a strategy to curb that behavior, a "stop" strategy.

When you find yourself making a bad habit, stop doing it right away by saying "stop." It can be useful to write STOP on a card with colored letters and have it on hand to look at it when you find yourself running that bad habit.

d) Replace the habit with an alternative behavior

When a habit involves the use of a part of the body, it is very useful to try to occupy it with an alternative activity so that it is incompatible with the bad habit. Although this involves doing something annoying, and even unpleasant to look at, it is an important step to eradicate the bad habit.

Another option is to think about the feeling that invades you when you are going to do what you want to eradicate and think about something that helps you dissipate that previous feeling. It may also be useful to develop skills that help you cope with situations that cause a bad habit. It all depends on what habit you want to eradicate.

e) Persist in being consistent and track progress

Consistency and persistence are the two most important measures to break the habit of intervention. If you work hard the first week, but then loosen up, you cannot eradicate the bad habit.

Be constant and control all the steps to weaken the habit.

You may at some point, feel that you cannot get it, which is too much for you. That is why it is important that you establish a system of rewards to strengthen yourself and that you continue thinking about the advantages that you will get when you get it.

f) Learn to manage lapses

Habits tend to repeat until they are completely broken. Since they are automatic, they tend to re-emerge. Therefore, you will have to make a great effort to break them completely to avoid this repetition.

The more you try, the better the chances of your bad habit disappear. What bad habits have you ended? If you are trying to get out of a bad habit, we encourage you to persist. After eliminating it from your life, you will feel full of joy.

15.3 Build Good Habits To Live Better

People often think that their identity and character traits determine their lifestyle. It is a belief that belongs, for example, to those who do not carry out physical activity because they feel they are too lazy, or to those who feel uncomfortable with the chaos of their own spaces but claim to be untidy and unable to do anything about it.

In reality, it is not the characteristics of your person that define your actions, but exactly the opposite: What you do today determines who you will be tomorrow. Regardless of what thoughts and beliefs you have about you, the possibility of choosing your future and achieving useful goals depends on you, on what you do and on your way of acting.

The only thing you can keep under your control are the actions.

To live better and increase the quality of your life, therefore, it is necessary to build positive processes, what we commonly call good habits. These are constructive actions that your brain is literally used to perceiving as rewarding and that it has learned to perform with a minimum level of effort, in energy-saving mode, often without being able to notice it

Develop good daily habits

Each of us has good habits but also develops bad ones, which affect our lifestyle. To be clear, I'm sure you happened to put your smartphone on the table and, without realizing it in the least, find it again in your hands while you scrub the social message boards with your finger. Here is a case of bad habit: an example of an action that the brain automatically performs as a response to a stimulus, in this case, boredom, and that makes you feel a momentary sense of gratification for having committed time successfully, albeit in a way non-constructive.

Forming new habits that are good for you allows you to bring order into your life and focus every day on building positive processes, which will become the certainties around which your everyday life revolves. It is a matter of living according to a flexible discipline, which will always leave a door opens to the beautiful innovations, to the sudden events that bring joy and benefit.

It is like having roots firmly planted in the ground: you will live with the awareness of which are the unshakable foundations on which to develop a resistant and stable trunk, impossible to shake, able to reach the sky with its vigorous branches in time.

Having control of daily actions strengthens you, restores your safety and makes you capable of facing life head-on, lightening the anxiety of waiting for answers about your future: you will be in fact acting yourself to find them or create them.

Three features to develop good habits

Since creating good habits is so important, I share with you the three fundamental aspects that you can acquire and develop to do it: commitment, constancy, and consistency.

Commitment is essential when you decide to change your habits. It is not enough to know and know, but it is necessary to combine all this in practice and add, through direct experience, the element of knowing how to do. It is only by rolling up your sleeves and passing to the work that you will realize what you desire. Furthermore, the commitment will be your best friend at the beginning and will help you overcome the period in which the road will be uphill, and you will feel the fatigue, the enormous effort due to your own resistance, the desire to give in and look back. By engaging, however, many things will begin to become spontaneous, automatic, and you will notice that the effort will be less while maintaining the desire to give the maximum and, why not, increasing the level of challenge.

At some point, you will have the feeling that the results you have hoped for, so you put yourself to work are slow in coming. You will feel the urge to throw in the towel, to give in and leave the path by sending the whole discourse of habits to the devil. However, be consistent! It takes time to form new processes, and it is good to stay focused on the path rather than the goal. He advances in small steps which, step by step, will give you long-term benefits, and not simply an ephemeral sense of "throw-away" satisfaction, such as that obtained because of bad habits. Do not give up, therefore, because the goal is not far away and by practicing constancy, you will be able to see it on the horizon and reach it.

Often, finally, habits are built that are not in line with one's dreams and with the image of oneself that one wishes to achieve.

When you make a choice to change habits and carry it forward, ask yourself if you are respecting your identity and the values that represent you with your actions. Are you yourself? Are you acting according to what you believe, in the name of your authenticity? If necessary, adjust the shot starting from listening to you and your way of being.

Feeling consistent with yourself and with what you believe makes you an integrated person and helps to increase your self-esteem, as well as to perceive largely the value you are creating in your life because you hear it resonate with all aspects of your existence.

15.4 Habits of Highly Successful Person

1. **the habit of setting clear and concrete goals leads to success**

It is said that he/she who does not know where it is going is probably going elsewhere. Goals are a navigation map for life. They are authentic when they are born of desire. They involve self-knowledge, reflection, and value.

Setting goals becomes a habit when faced with each situation you choose a course. Do not let circumstances lead you, but look to the point and define where you want to go.

2. **Understand the motivations**

Motivations are a key factor in successful people. To have a why and for what gives the strength and the decision to reach its objectives. In many cases, the definition of reasons and purposes is a good indicator of independence of judgment and honesty towards oneself.

What gives meaning to a goal is its reason for being. We are used to looking for reasons to achieve it or not. It may be the difference between success or not. If there is no why or no definite purpose, it is difficult to find motives or reasons that sustain the strength to persevere.

3. Make timely decisions

Any decision requires courage because it always has disadvantages and benefits. It also implies a risk: what resolves can lead to success or failure. In this case, to decide is one of those things that sometimes shake us up to our foundations.

Successful people do not delegate their decisions or feel embarrassed when they have no one to give them advice or advice on what to do. They understand that it is they, and they alone, who must assume their determination and its consequences. This does not prevent them from asking for help when needed.

4. Manage time properly

Time is perhaps more precious than life. He is life itself. Successful people know that time is running out and that's why you have to make the most of it. This implies managing it on the basis of a clearly defined and articulated scale of priorities.

People get used to prioritizing or not doing. They have the habit of shifting everything at the last moment, or of doing it with enough margin to scuttle the goal by poisoning it from the first unforeseen. They also distribute their hours constructively and intelligently. This means that they are able to find the time to be good in their work, but also to take care of their families (and take care of them).

5. Seize opportunities to improve

Laziness and success never go together. To succeed, it is necessary to have at least one point of requirement towards oneself. If the goal is to grow and go far, it is essential to develop some skill by taking advantage of opportunities, or even generating them in their absence. This applies on any plane: intellectual, physical or emotional.

In addition, success requires a certain amount of humility to accept that we can always be better. It is also necessary to point out that there is little chance of doing this alone, although chance can contribute a lot. Think that a successful person is used to looking for options to grow.

6. Focusing to reach the goal

Dispersion leads only to endure in a state of confusion and doubt. it illustrates that what is desired is not clear enough. And if you do not know what you want, you'll have a hard time getting it. In fact, it is difficult to advance.

When you start many things but do not finish any, you are just wasting your time. Successful people are used to finishing all that they propose to do. They know that this in itself is a success.

7. Respect the rest periods

The body, the soul and the spirit need moments of relaxation and fulfillment. We are whole beings and nourish only one of our facets takes us, sooner or later, to pour us out. Rest and recreation are ways to respect our human integrity.

It's one thing to definitely focus on one achievement and another very different from becoming obsessed with it. Rest helps us recover energy and take a step back from what is usual to better distinguish it. Remember that those who know how to spend their free time are more likely to achieve their goals more effectively.

CHAPTER SIXTEEN: Personal Mastery And Improving Your Life

There are a lot of people who have recently discovered personal mastery as a method that could improve their way of life and deepen their perspective and outlook What is personal mastery and how can it improve your life?

Personal or Self mastery is about deepening our understanding and expanding our perspective about life. It develops vision, energies and enables us to determine what direction we are taking in our life. People who have achieved this mastery testified that they would feel a positive change in their life.

There are different benefits an individual may gain from personal mastery:

- Clear decision making - since an individual who have attained mastery has gained clear vision on their purpose and their mission in life, decision making would be easy and at the same clear for them.

- Strong creative leadership - personal mastery develops strong leadership, also can develop a person's communication skills and confidence as a leader. Effective leaders also need to manage their emotions and not let their emotions get in the way of making judgment.

- Increased emotion intelligence - mastering our emotions could be difficult at times especially during period of difficult and challenging times. Coaching and counseling could improve how an individual develop and master their emotions.

- Improved work life balance - those who have attained mastery testified that they can see significant effect on how they have handled their life. What's good with personal mastery is that you can implement this even in your career and interpersonal relationship.

- Reduced stress levels - since personal mastery deals with understanding reality and weaknesses, it can result in lower stress levels. Aside from that, mastery over one's self also helps an individual accept change and be flexible about it. This could help a person deal with stress and reduce it.

This type of self improvement can even help you let go of bad habits and behaviour. For example, personal mastery can help you get over with smoking or alcoholic addiction. You do not only address the habit but deals with the reason why you have started the habit in the first place. The difference is when you only address the habit, it is possible for it to come back again. But when you tackle the issues behind the habit, it would make you stop the habit altogether.

One of the great things about self mastery is that it can be applied whether you want to improve your career, leadership or your organization. self mastery can even help you with career, whether you would like to change your path or would like to improve your performance in the current career you are in.

Business organizations have cited different benefits when their leaders and their members have achieved personal mastery. Studies and statistics showed that companies and business organization were able to think creatively about resolving issues. Self mastery were also able to bring out the best from the employees and also able to have higher staff retention. Employers also comment on the strong relationship among the workers, personal mastery could encompass teams, departments and even workers and senior relationship. Business statistics also showed that mastery over one's self showe's an increase in productivity, profit and customer service performance.

Personal mastery, contrary to what it literally means, is not just for your own person. Improving yourself could mean a lot, you are a part of a whole (another personal mastery key principle). Your improvement can influence others and eventually change the world into something better.

16.1 Effective Tricks To Have New Habits

1. Have a good reason to establish that habit.

Why do you want to establish that new habit? Or rather, what for? Are you convinced by your own reasons? If your own reasons don't convince you, the best thing you can do is look for reasons that convince you or decide not to establish that habit.

Who do you think will get before spending a day watching movies in English every day? Anyone who next year goes around the world or someone whose parents insist that knowing English is important today?

It is very important that the habit you want to establish is aligned with your values and your expectations.

2. Tell everyone.

Tell as many people as possible your intention to establish the new habit, so in addition to the commitment to yourself, you will also have it in some sense with others.

You don't feel like telling people you paid a year of a gym membership to go just two days right? Telling people about your intentions can generate positive social pressure, as well as a support and motivation group.

3. Imagine how you will feel with that new habit.

It is more than proven that immediate consequences have more weight on our behaviors and decisions than long-term consequences.

Do you think someone would eat a chocolate cake if in each bite he gained 100 grams of weight? Right? The problem is that the pastries, in general, are very rich at this time (immediate consequence) and the harmful effects of eating it constantly (such as weight gain) are not seen until after a while.

For this reason, it is important to be able to bring these future benefits to the present through visualization. If you are able to imagine how your life will improve and how good you will feel thanks to your new habit, I assure you that you will be much more motivated for change.

4. Condition that habit to a temporary external signal.

Find a sign or reminder that drives you to take immediate action. For example, go to the gym after work or just get up. Or set a time at which an alarm will sound and you will stop doing whatever you are doing to get to exercise the new habit.

This way it will be easier for the habit to be automated and more complicated to make excuses for not putting it into practice. There will come a time when it will seem that one activity pushes you to the other, just as it happens to me in the morning when it seems that the alarm prompts me to go directly to the shower.

5. Help yourself with external elements.

The willpower is not infinite so do not hesitate to help in external elements all you can.

What is wrong with using a walker before learning to walk? External control is a previous step to self-control

If you want to eat healthily, do not buy junk food, paste your daily menu in the fridge and photos of how your new version will be with 5kg less.

If you want to quit smoking, stay away from the snuff boxes, the terraces of the bars and at least during the first days of your smoking friends.

6. Change the way you talk to yourself and others.

If you have quit smoking, you are not trying, and you are a non-smoker.

If you are eating healthier, you are not starting a diet, and you have opted for a healthy lifestyle.

If you are studying languages you are not making your first steps, and you are studying a new language seriously.

7. Little by little.

If you have exercised in life, you don't think about going to the gym for the first day and a half and getting into a Crossfit class since the safest thing is that the next day you can't even move and crawl to cancel your subscription thinking that is not your thing.

It is recommended that you elaborate an action plan in which you determine what the starting point is, how far you want to go and what is the minimum you will do (this can always be modified as you go along) and what are the steps to follow to reach there.

8. Be concrete.

When you want to establish a new habit (or leave an old one), you not only have to be clear why you want to do it but what exactly you want to do.

For example, it is not the same to say I want to lead a healthier life that I will replace the fried ones with boiled and grilled foods and go for a run 30 min three days a week. The more concrete your habit is, the more likely you will successfully install it.

9. Never stop practicing the new habit two days in a row.

At least during the phase of establishment and consolidation of the habit, it is important that they never spend two days in a row without you practicing it. One day an unforeseen may arise, not two days in a row.

So if there is something you should postpone and leave for another day, other than your new habit. If you find difficulty in achieving it or if you look very rushed in time, then reduce the action in time and / or intensity.

10. Reward your progress.

Strengthen your progress. Do something you like after exercising the habit, give yourself little whims to celebrate your progress, talk to yourself recognizing your effort, and with positive words

16.2 Habits You Should Have In Your Life

The meditation:

The lifestyle of this century makes many people live accelerated and suffer anxiety problems.

It is enough that you feel in a comfortable position and focus solely and exclusively on your breathing. Few minutes of meditation a day can give you more benefits than you imagine. Try it for a month and tell me.

An adequate diet:

Body and mind are indivisible concepts. If you take care of your body, you are taking care of your mind and vice versa. A supply adequate with less refined sugar and more vegetables will make you feel much better. I know it sounds like a tope, but it's a truth like a cathedral.

Do sports:

It has been shown that doing sports causes us to release endorphins, hormones that among other functions, are responsible for providing feelings of well-being. Exercising is the best anxiolytic and antidepressant that exists.

Read every day:

How about spending 30 minutes before going to sleep to read books of interest? Reading develops concentration, creativity, and imagination.

In addition, if you manage to establish this habit of reading, you will not only learn a lot of new things but also enjoy a better quality dream since you will divert the view of screens and elements that can activate your physiology by spoiling your sleep quality.

Spend time caring for your social relationships:

A dinner with your partner on Saturday nights? A coffee with friends on Sundays?

Several studies point out that the levels of perceived happiness correlate directly with the quality of our social relationships. In addition, people who have quality social relationships live longer and have lower rates of depression.

CHAPTER SEVENTEEN: The Art of Communicating As A Couple

It is important to keep in mind that most of the mistakes made in the couple's communication have to do with not knowing how to express themselves properly or for trying to impose our criteria or for disrespecting the other person. On many occasions, the couple wants to be as we wish without being interested in their views or beliefs. When it comes to forming a couple, all people have expectations about the relationship, and the problem comes when they are not realistic, or the couple does not know or share them.

Many times, without being aware, we impose our expectations, how we expect our partner to behave with us. Through therapy and couples, we seek to reach meeting points, a territory, landscape, or map where both members can meet their needs and continue walking hand in hand.

- Active listening is a fundamental key that implies accepting the emotions of the other person, not judging, not trying to solve the problem (advice is given only when the other person asks for it and after listening) and not interrupting

- Always speak from the self and from how I feel instead of using you that encourages the other person to become defensive

- Ask and listen before throwing yourself to accuse. It is important to clear up all confusion without accusations.

- Substitute the demands for requests, and we don't like anyone to force us

- Increase positive interactions with your partner. Couples want to argue less.

- Treat the couple with love and kindness, couples who have a greater number of positive interactions such as caresses, smiles, hugs, compliments, surprises and willingness to listen develop better communication

- When our partner gives us good news, respond by showing joy before the enthusiasm of our partner and ask questions about it so that our partner feels we are interested.

- Make a critical analysis of the failures we have in communication, not only in what the couple should change

- It is important not to shut things up and face all problems and misunderstandings with assertive, respectful, and open communication. To avoid reproaches, it is important to stop accumulating resentment (now I don't tell you anything, but I will return it to you), it is important that everything can be spoken with love and respect, in due course. If we use silence as a weapon or as a way to avoid conflict, that will make the couple feel belittled, attacked, and humiliated, and that brings many negative feelings that often awaken verbal aggression.

- Actively listen, realize the emotion we are feeling, think about how our partner may feel, and the consequences of saying what arises spontaneously and before judging, ask.

- Empathize, ask us the question if I were to receive my speech"… how would I take it? Putting ourselves in the place of the couple helps us to self-regulate our emotions

- Find the right time to address problems, a time where you are calm, and there is no interference from the environment, or you are not excessively tired or hungry, etc. It is important to keep in mind that hurries or conversations by WhatsApp are our worst enemies.

- Go topic by topic, trying to avoid getting many things at once. It is important to be specific, to focus on possible solutions.

- Most discussions are caused by misunderstandings, and each person has a way of perceiving the world, which, instead of judging or assuming, it is important that we ask. As much as we connect our partner, we cannot guess the thoughts, feelings, and intentions of another person

- Generalizations are all phrases that begin or contain "always," "never," "never," we must be careful not to Tag, our partner when we address a topic. It is always better to talk about concrete facts and not label our partner. "

- When you feel very angry and want to hurt the couple, it is often better to spend time outside and wait to calm down so we can speak well.

- Nonverbal communication is key because not everything is said in words. A sincere smile, a sympathetic look can be keys to handling a conflict

Another aspect in the couple is that when there is a conflict in the couple, it is very important to focus not so much on the facts but on the emotions, the unmet needs, and feelings behind each person. It is very useful to ask people how they feel and what they would need. When we discuss it is useful to be humble and to be able to show our own mistakes, even though they are infinitely smaller than those of my partner. Timely withdrawal prevents escalation of the conflict. It is important that we keep in mind that as a couple, it is better to form a team and not compete.

On many occasions, vicious circles are generated in the communication, for example, one of the two members of the couple is very quiet, and when they can no longer, it bursts into accusations; the other member then receives a storm of reproaches and avoids discussion, runs away from the situation, that in turn causes the other person to get angrier and the more angry, the more the other person closes and the more one closes, the other gets angry, etc.

Thus vicious circles are formed in the couple. Unfortunately, we have not been trained for life as a couple with which people are creating habits and automatisms and changing it on many occasions requires the help of a professional who will also guide the couple to manage the resentment and reproaches of the past. Working communication in the couple is worthwhile and helps us to improve all personal relationships in general.

CHAPTER EIGHTEEN: Zoom Out To Take Perspective, the Art Of Reflecting From A Distance

One way to relieve anxiety and make more authentic contact with our self and its needs is by distancing ourselves. Now, to do so you don't have to take a plane. Sometimes, a long walk alone is enough to calm the mind and 'see better'.

Sometimes, it is worth moving away to take perspective and distance ourselves temporarily from what is close to us, to decide better, to clarify ideas, desires, emotions. Achieving it is not always easy, since most of us are very attached to that immediate reality so full of stimuli and pressures. However, performing this exercise can be highly beneficial.

There is a fact that, no doubt, is curious. People are skilled experts in distancing ourselves almost every moment, but yes, we do it through that hyper-erratic but wandering mind, which is often lost in their own maze of worries, ruminant thoughts and memories. These types of mental processes do not help, are not useful and often place us in states of great exhaustion.

Daniel Goleman reminded us in his Focus book the need to train attention. Thus, and as striking as it may seem, one way to achieve this is to apply another type of distance. We refer to that in which the brain is able to lift the anchor of the useless and immediate mental rumor, to be placed in a watchtower of silence in which to look where it is important.

Let's see below how to get it.

"The control of emotional life and its subordination to an objective is essential to spur and maintain attention, motivation and creativity."

-Daniel Goleman-

Walking away to take perspective, key to decide better

From the field of psychology a new term is emerging that is worth taking into account: we refer to self-differentiation. It is an interesting concept that reverts, for example, in a better management of stress and anxiety, in a more effective decision-making and even in an exceptional way to enhance the creative process.

This technique already has several studies, such as the one carried out in the Department of Psychology at the University of California in 2018. Doctors Michael Duckworth and Al Kross pointed out that simply resting your eyes in a relaxing but attractive setting helps us to distance ourselves psychically from the immediate reality to connect with ourselves. It is a strategy of autosuggestion .

Therefore, moving away to take perspective does not necessarily imply having to pack. It is not necessary to travel several kilometers to establish a physical separation from our daily life and from our surroundings . Sometimes, learning to train mental distance will undoubtedly offer us a large number of almost unexpected benefits.

The art of seeing the world in second person

If there is something that we tend to influence often from the field of psychology, it is the need to learn to be present. Also in the importance of tuning in with our thoughts and needs. Now, sometimes, it is necessary to move away to take perspective and one way to do it is to see ourselves and the world in second person.

And what is the point? We will ask. It is an ideal mechanism to reduce the noise of emotions. It is being able to speak with kindness, but directly. In turn, it allows us to analyze our inner world with objectivity, calmness and full awareness. To achieve this, nothing better than going to a quiet place and having an internal dialogue that can follow these guidelines:

- What worries you (we'll say our name)?

- So what do you think is best for you now?

- What can you do to fix it?

Remember that you deserve to be happy, you have to be brave. Everything will be fine.

Self-differentiation is a way to deactivate for a moment the egocentric talk and thus evaluate our reality in a more calm and distanced emotional state of the central "I".

The psychological distance as a tool of well-being

Who chooses to move away to take perspective does not need to put many kilometers in between. Sometimes, not even going to the other side of a continent helps us to avoid worries and problems; We have that clear. Now, what will really help us is to exercise psychological distance.

This term, that of psychological distance, has several studies that support its benefit in terms of mental health. Dr. Yaacov Thope, a professor of psychology at the University of New York , did an interesting job explaining the following:

Sometimes, it is necessary to go beyond our 'I' beyond the here and now. It is about bringing our mind to a state of calm that allows us to relativize moments of stress and high pressure. It is also a way that certain circumstances, behaviors or stimuli do not affect us too much.

That psychological distance allows us to have a healthier dialogue with ourselves. That is to say phrases like 'don't let this affect you', 'think it's the best for you, decide something that will generate well-being'...

To conclude, sometimes, moving away to take perspective reverses directly in our psychological balance. We can do it mentally and, in fact, if we train in this practice we will be able to handle stressful situations better every day. However, and as we well know, from time to time the physical distance, such as a trip, is also as therapeutic as it is enriching.

18.1 What Does Distance Mean In Your Life

Having adequate distance management in our lives means implementing the necessary actions to approach what we want to keep close and put the barriers of the case if what we are looking for is to move away or move away.

Distance is a physical concept that in the case of the human being has psychological implications. Proof of this are those colloquial expressions of everyday use such as "keep the distances ", "be close" or "approach" someone. There is also talk of "distancing" from situations, or "moving away" from what affects us.

In physical terms, the issue of distance is also very relevant for the human being. Everyone has their own spaces and addresses them specifically. We need different degrees of physical distance in our social relationships. Also an individual vital space, because all this has implications in our life.

" Cell phones help to be connected to those who are at a distance. Cell phones allow those who connect... stay away . "

-Zygmunt Bauman-

Distance is a concept that also applies to objects and their effect on the human psyche . The sensation generated by a room with many crowded objects is different from that

FROM EMPATHY TO EMOTIONAL MANAGEMENT

produced by another, where there are few things, distant from each other. Let's look at all this more carefully.

Physical distance and its effects

Distance finds its most evident form of expression on the physical plane. Distance or physical approach is a manifestation of distance or emotional approach . This is not only evidenced in the distance or proximity between the body of one person and the other, it is also expressed in gestures, tones of voice and postures.

Researchers Lawrence E. Williams and John A. Bargh, the first from the University of Colorado and the second from Yale University, conducted an intensive study on the subject. They concluded that " perceptual and motor representations of physical distance influence people's thoughts and feelings."

This means that physical distance influences judgments and emotional states of people. In their investigation, Williams and Bargh encouraged some people to take physical distance from people who were very close to them before. Over time they showed that this distance had affected their attachment to them.

The distance and the conflict

The conclusions reached by investigators Lawrence E. Williams and John A. Bargh have repercussions on different aspects, including that of the conflict. One of the results of his experiments indicates that " feelings of distance can moderate the emotional intensity of stimuli ." In other words, what is far affects us less.

This proves that this measure of taking physical distance from what affects us negatively is effective . The distance leads to the influence of that person, or that situation, to moderate. Therefore, it helps the feelings decrease in intensity and, instead, there is a more dispassionate perspective. Moving away physically from conflictive people or spaces helps to clarify those conflicts.

However, in humans, and even in animals, proximity and distance are also an emotional and mental issue . You can be physically away from something or someone and, however, the loop can be even narrower and more intense than if we were one centimeter away. And the opposite is also true: we are physically close to something or someone, but, at the same time, light years away from that.

The distance in the subjective world

If we want to cut ties with something or someone, physical distance is only the first step. Yes or yes it will significantly alter the link we have with that reality. What is not going to happen is to cut it definitively, depending on the remoteness itself. For this to happen, it is necessary that an emotional distance is also constructed.

If we want to have emotional proximity with someone, we must also have physical closeness . This implies being physically present in your life. With the presence itself, but also with physical closeness, that is, with hugs, words, caresses , etc. Emotional closeness, meanwhile, involves having that person in mind and approaching your inner world, through conversation.

At the same time, if the goal is to distance ourselves from someone, we must do the corresponding thing. That is, physically move away first. Not being there with a present body, but also not making a presence surreptitiously, that is, spying on that person or keeping abreast of his life, or constantly thinking about it. This contributes to putting the emotional distance of the case, that is, a cut with its influence on our life.

CHAPTER NINETEEN: Emotional And Rational Empathy, How Do They Manifest In Our Brains?

One of the most powerful tools that human beings use to understand the multiple social changes we have experienced in recent years is empathy. Empathizing gives us a totally incredible cognitive ability when we know how to use it properly for the benefit of all.

Empathizing is that act by which a person identifies and understands the feelings of another person, taking into account the specific circumstances of the other person, and acts accordingly. Empathy is possible thanks to the great power that our mind has to separate our feelings from those of others and even use a different way of reasoning depending on the "sentimental place" in which it is being put.

This allows us to adapt to the environment, understanding as a means fundamentally to our environment and people around us. Empathy allows someone to feel close to the pain or suffering of another person but also to their joy or happiness. But do we all empathize equally?

«If you are not able to control your stressful emotions, if you cannot have empathy and have effective personal relationships, no matter how intelligent you are, you will not get very far.»

-Daniel Goleman-

Empathy generates changes in our brain

There are many of us who still ask ourselves the question "do we all empathize in the same way and intensity?" The answer is no: studies tell us that we differentiate ourselves in terms of our level of empathy. In addition, we can say that somehow not everyone travels the same paths to empathize. There are people who have a great relationship with their emotional world and somehow it is more natural for them to do so.

Others do not have this "gift," or at least they do not have it as developed. Therefore, they generate their empathy through experience and even their own sentimental "logic and coherence." Thus, according to research from the University of Monash (Australia) it has been discovered that the brains of rational or logical people are physically different from those of the most emotional people.

The head of the research team Robert Eres states that "the people who have high levels of emotional empathy are often those who feel quite scared when they watch a horror movie, or start crying during a sad scene. On the contrary, those with high cognitive empathy are more rational ».

The objective of this research was that empathy generates changes in our body, based on our brain and distinguishing two types:

- Affective empathy is the ability of the person to respond properly to the emotional state of another.

- Cognitive empathy consists in the ability to understand and feel what the other person is developing or thinking.

Affective empathy and cognitive empathy

The study was conducted with 176 participants who measured with voxel-based morphometry, the amount of gray matter that they had in certain regions of the brain. The result of the scientific work has been published by the journal NeuroImage in which the results reveal that people with emotional empathy have a greater density of gray matter in the brain region of the island, located in the central part of our brain.

FROM EMPATHY TO EMOTIONAL MANAGEMENT

On the other hand, people with high cognitive empathy possessed more gray matter in the cingulate gyrus, which we find in the middle area of the brain and allows us to carry out the basic brain functions of our limbic system.

According to the researchers, this work "provides the validation that empathy is a construction of multiple components, so that emotional and cognitive empathy are differentially represented in brain morphometry." With these data we can understand the physical complexity that exists in each of the brains, thus being able to answer the big question of "emotional and rational people, how do their brains differ?"

«When people talk, listen completely. Most people never listen. »

-Ernest Hemingway-

19.2 Oliver Sacks And The Secrets Of The Brain

Dr. P was a wonderful musician and went to Oliver Sacks' office because he seemed to have some vision problems. Sacks examined him and at the end of the visit Dr. P looked around him for the hat. He reached out and took his wife by the head trying to put it on. He confused his wife with a hat. What he had was a problem in his brain, not his sight

Oliver Sacks prescribed him to make music the whole of his life, because for Dr. P music had taken the place of the image and he was only able to do everyday activities such as dressing or eating while singing. This is just an example of the secrets of the human brain that Oliver Sacks unveiled throughout his life.

"Our memory is our coherence, our reason, our action, our feeling. Without her we are nothing…"

-Luis Buñuel-

Oliver Sacks has been one of the most recognized neurologists in the world, with works that have even been taken to the cinema as "Awakenings." Not only was he dedicated to studying the human brain, but he has been discovering his secrets in a close language and using the stories of his own patients, without losing scientific rigor. The merit of Sacks is to have achieved that the public understood easily concepts that in principle were reserved to the neurologists.

The secrets of the brain and music

One of the main phenomena that Oliver Sacks studied is the relationship between music and the brain. Both in his book "The man who confused his wife with a hat" - in the case we have seen at the beginning of the article - as in "Musicofilia", where he analyzes various cases of patients with brain disorders that nevertheless connect with the world Through music.

In the first part of "Musicofilia" (Possessed by music) Sacks analyzes cases in which music negatively affects some people because it becomes an obsession. This is the case of Tony Cicoria, a doctor outside of music who, after surviving lightning, develops a great fondness for piano that becomes an obsession. That obsession with music affected his professional life and his marriage in a very negative way.

"Every disease is a musical problem; every cure is a musical solution"

-Novalis-

In the second part of Musicofilia (A varied musicality), Sacks talks about cases of musical synesthesia, in which a person identifies notes or scales with colors or flavors. It also speaks of cases in which a person identifies a tone in an absolute way, that is, that he is able to identify a note perfectly.

In addition, Sacks highlights the connection between diseases such as Parkinson's and music as a means to mitigate its most uncomfortable manifestations, or as Tourette's syndrome whose spasms and tics seem to be controlled when the patient performs a musical activity. In the last part of the book "Emotion, identity and music", Sacks analyzes musical dreams and other interactions between the most sensitive aspects of each of us and music.

Therefore, the neurocognitive processing of music involves the interaction of various brain functions, both neuropsychological and emotional. Depending on what aspect of the music is analyzed (tone, temporal organization, sequence, etc.), different areas of the brain intervene.

Music as an emotional stimulus, activates different areas of the brain whether it is pleasant music (nucleus accumbens) or unpleasant (tonsil) for that reason, its use as therapy in certain diseases is so important.

The farewell of Oliver Sacks

Last August Oliver Sacks died at 82 in New York and left us his enormous contribution to neurology and literature. His reflections on the human brain, based on the analysis of real cases of patients who had come to his office over the years, has regained an ancient way of telling science. A form that separates from the statistics that currently dominates psychology and that somehow humanizes it, recognizing that in essence each case is unique.

In the month of February, after overcoming a melanoma in his eye, he publicly announced that the cancer had spread and that he had a few months to live. As a farewell, he wrote a column in The New York Times that moved the whole world and of which we transcribe a part:

«I have loved and I have been loved. I have been given a lot and I have given something in return, I have read and traveled and thought and written (...) Above all I have been a sensitive being, a thinking animal, on this beautiful planet. It has been a great adventure and a huge privilege »

-Oliver Sacks-

CHAPTER TWENTY: Reduce Anger To Develop Empathy

The anger is a widespread problem that we all experience. Managing anger is a somewhat complex skill that must be worked on. Although now we are not going to talk about how to handle it, but how to reduce it through the development of another fundamental skill: empathy. And empathy is crucial to reduce the intensity and frequency of anger attacks.

People with significant anger problems have difficulties with empathy and forgiveness. However, empathy is a skill that can be developed and cultivated over time. Empathy is partly unconscious and automatic, but it is also possible to make a conscious choice and develop it with practice.

Conscious empathy

The ability to feel empathy begins at the unconscious level. However, it can develop as a conscious skill when a person is able to understand the feelings and intentions of another person. Therefore, it is possible to retrain our brain and be more empathetic with effort and conscious practice.

For the development of empathy, the person's past experiences give an important clue that facilitates precise knowledge, helping to understand his inner world and his current state.

When someone is crying, you might think about your situation and the things that make you feel sad . And when you feel the pain of the other, you feel sad too. Everyone's experience is unique, so relating it to their own experience may not be enough: the other person may be sad for different reasons that you do not understand or about which you have no knowledge.

Free yourself to feel empathy

To be empathic, it is necessary to aerate our prejudices. In order to evaluate the pain of the other person, you have to reach it, know your life, attend to what you have to say, listen to your feelings and keep a full attention in the course of the conversation.

Once the person opens, you may be able to know what exactly is bothering you. This type of empathy requires a special type of connection. A channel that sometimes costs a lot to open but that becomes more fluid with practice.

In this context, it is important to understand that empathy also implies the understanding of thoughts and actions , and not just emotions. To be empathic it is necessary to go beyond feelings and also understand the way of thinking, intentions and perception about the other person's world.

This is what is called empathic concern . People who are empathic also tend to show greater empathic concern for other people.

Therefore, if you are angry with another person, and you want to reduce the intensity of such anger, you need to develop both skills: empathy and empathic concern . Empathy reduces anger, as it eliminates negative judgments . For its part, empathic concern also reduces anger, because the responses take into account the needs of the other, and help reduce those visceral reactions that characterize the attacks of anger.

Understand each other

In essence, empathy is a skill that can be developed and improved. When it is achieved, a better understanding of the inner world of the other person is acquired . Thanks to empathy, anger can be reduced because you can feel more sensitive to the difficulties, problems or situations that affect the other.

There is a negative correlation between empathy and anger. Anger tends to decrease a person's ability to be empathic. But if you show empathy with the other person, chances are you don't get mad at that person. Thus, empathy tends to inhibit anger and aggression, facilitating understanding and giving coherence to the behaviors of others.

Coherence? Yes, something that has nothing to do with justification but with the compression of the reasons that produce a behavior . Thus, for example, understanding the reactions that motivate an aggression can help prevent it from happening again.

The ability to calm down

Keep in mind that anger makes people have a hard time calming down. And calm is crucial for empathy , in order to effectively understand each other's thoughts, feelings and intentions. Thus, by showing empathy with the other person, violent reactions can be reduced.

When the person is angry and his heart is beating very hard, it is difficult to take into account the person's thoughts, feelings and intentions. This, in turn, intensifies anger and causes the other person to be misjudged. That makes this person assigned a label, so all their actions will be seen in the light of that mistaken belief. That is why it is also important to work on your labels and be more objective to cultivate empathy and empathic concern.

On the other hand, angry people tend to multiply their hostility because they feel the desire to punish those who have made them angry. Instead of trying to comfort the other party, they show that anger and hostility and want revenge. This interferes with empathic concern. In this sense, some people manifest anger as a way to avoid feeling sad about someone else's pain.

Differences in the ways of reacting

There are individual differences in how people can cope with anger provocations and aggressive reactions. Some people have a better ability to handle another person's anger. They have a greater capacity to perceive pain, shame, guilt, sadness, loneliness and fears that make them angry.

These people are able to put themselves in their shoes and understand their perspective, control their reactions and empathize with the person who is angry. They can relate better to the angry person and have a better ability to get along with others.

However, other people are more sensitive and internalize anger a lot. They also tend to withdraw from what is unpleasant for them, inhibiting the expression of their feelings and, therefore, moving away from assertive communication.

The key to reducing anger

Once we develop the ability to understand the pain of others and the underlying dynamics of another person's anger behaviors, it is easier to cope with that reaction and get along with it.

Being defensive and justifying anger can be counterproductive and will not make you an empathetic person. Try to listen to other people's feelings and show sensitivity towards others to develop empathy and empathic concern.

Life is too short to waste because of being constantly angry and aggressive. Revenge or feeling above others does not lead to any good place. To manage to control that anger that this type of circumstances and others causes, the key lies in developing the necessary skills in dealing with others.

www.ingramcontent.com/pod-product-compliance
Lightning Source LLC
Chambersburg PA
CBHW061346250726
48657CB00004B/1349